SMART SKETCH BOOK 1

Oogie Art's step-by-step guide to pencil drawing for beginners.

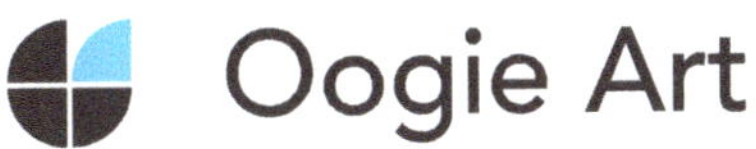

Oogie Art's SmartSketchbook™
An Expert's Guide to Still Life in Pencil
First Edition, Copyright © 2015

Produced and Edited by
Oogie Art
New York, NY

Directed by
Wook Choi

Assistant Directed by
Clara Lu

Drawings by
Jee Hwang

Tips by
Wook Choi

Published and Distributed by
Oogie Publishing House
New York, NY
www.oogiepublishinghouse.com
(212) 714-1011

ISBN 978-0-9855809-2-6
Printed in the United States

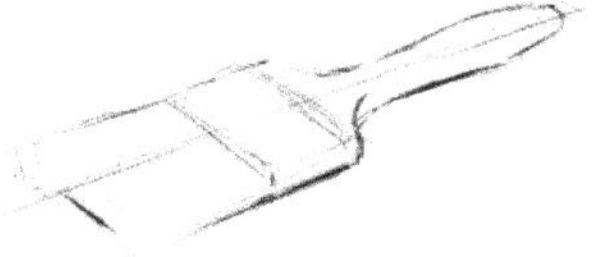
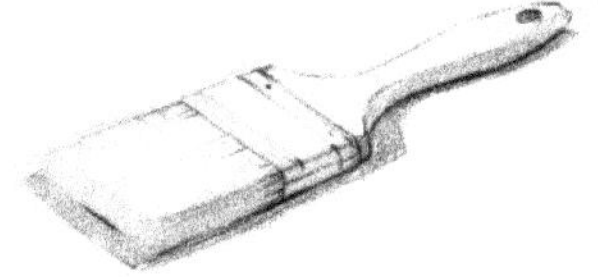
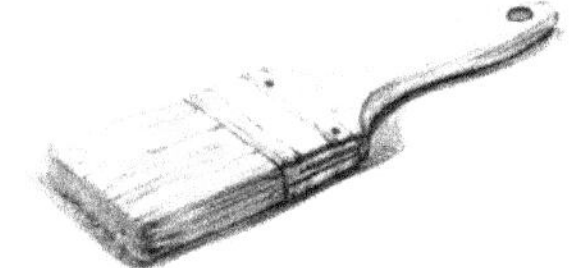
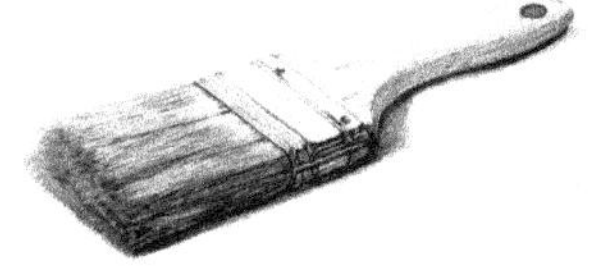

CONTENTS

Introduction to Pencil

Pencils are the tools most often associated with drawing. They are versatile, sensual, fluid, and mistakes are easy to correct with an eraser. Pencils are, however, unforgiving in that even the slightest pressure will leave a mark; senstivity is certainly a required skill.

Complete the beginning exercises on the next few pages to develop the sensitivity you will need to master the pencil.

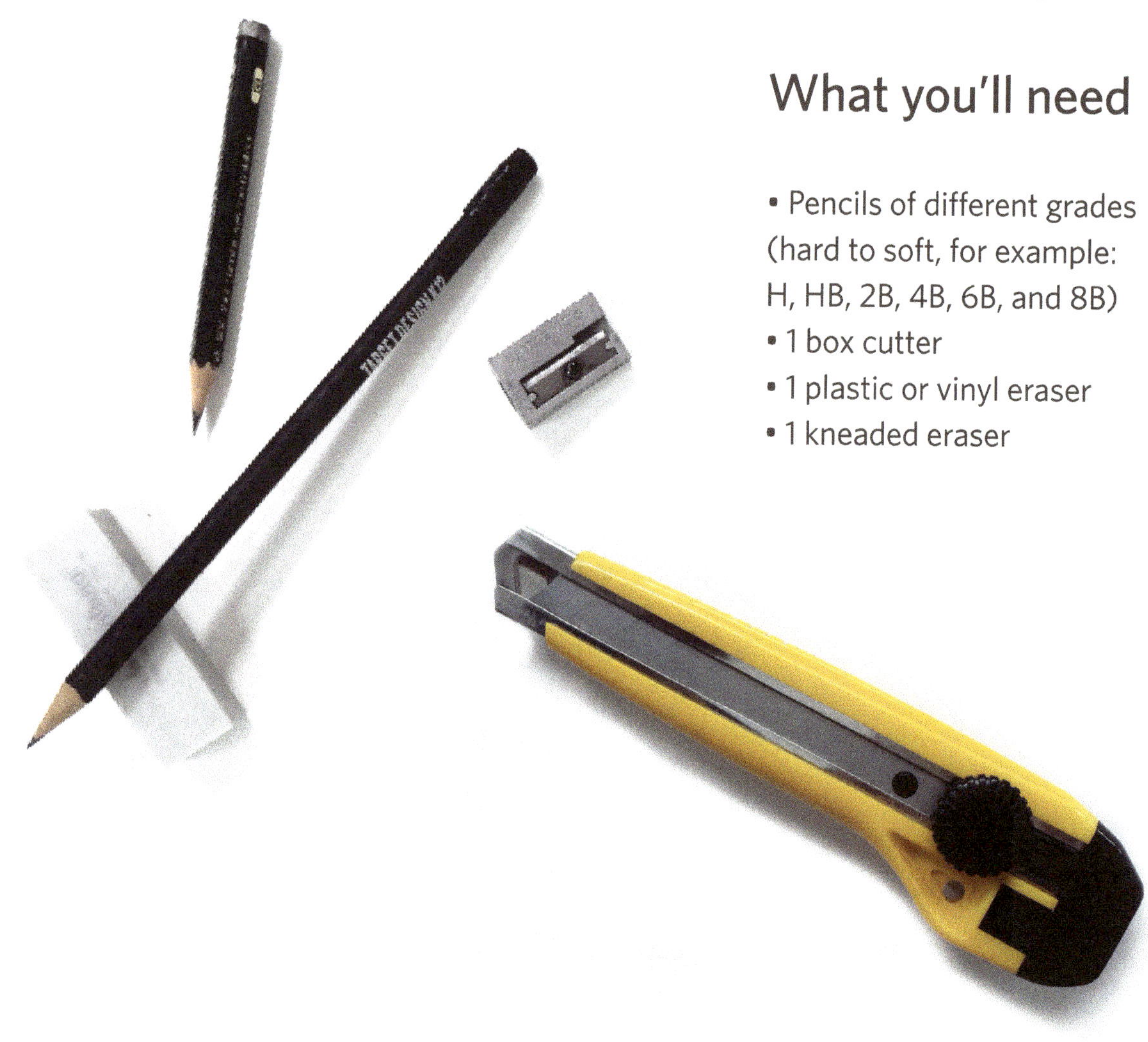

What you'll need

- Pencils of different grades (hard to soft, for example: H, HB, 2B, 4B, 6B, and 8B)
- 1 box cutter
- 1 plastic or vinyl eraser
- 1 kneaded eraser

Box Cutter

In mastering the pencil, it is also very important to know how to use your other tools, including the very important box cutter. The box cutter helps to create a sharp pencil with a point that will not break, which typically happens with regular pencil sharpeners. It also helps in cutting your eraser when you need a sharp edge for creating highlights in your drawings.

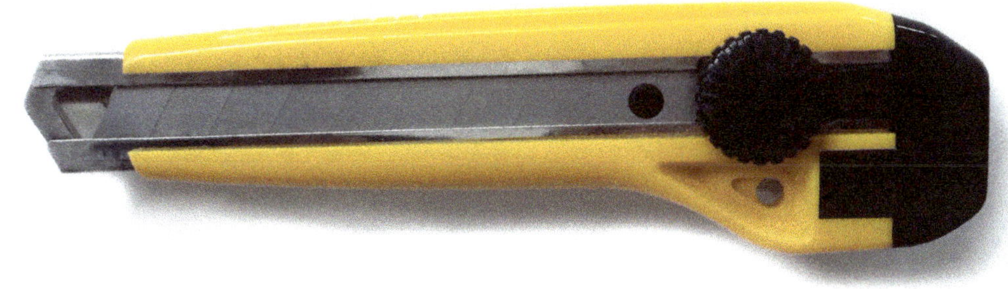

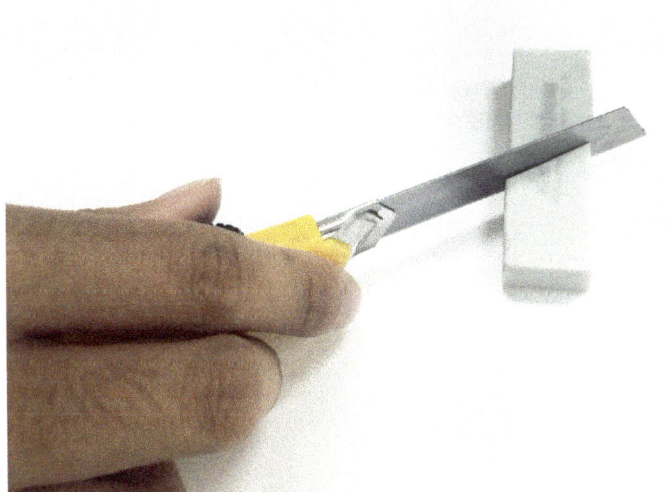

Cut the eraser at around a 60 degree angle for using the sharp edges for highlights and cleaning edges, textures, etc.

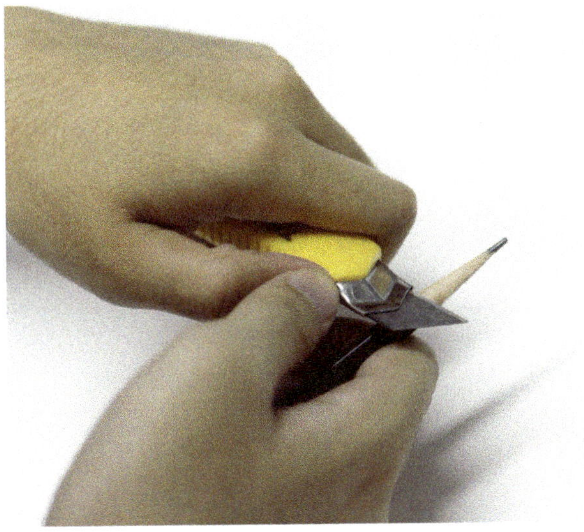

Stabilizing the pencil in your right hand, hold the box cutter in your left hand and place it perpendicular to the pencil. Push the blade along the pencil as shown to sharpen the pencil. The longer the blade strokes, the more stabilized the point will be.

Grip and Pressure

The right way to hold a pencil is to place the thumbnail perpendicular to your face. Adjust the pressure power of the thumb rather than the index finger to control the intensity of your marks.

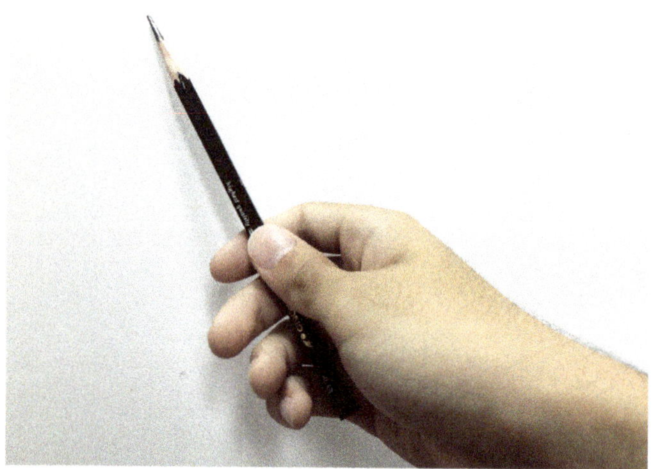

Hold the pencil at the end and rest the pencil lightly on the paper to create soft lines for defining general shapes and outlines in laying out the composition. This grip will allow you to create gentle lines without using too much pressure and making dark lines that are hard to erase.

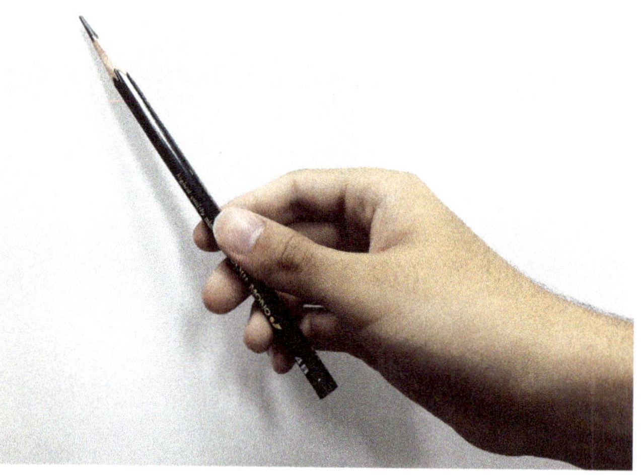

Position your fingers in the middle of the pencil for more control; this position is for drawing strong lines.

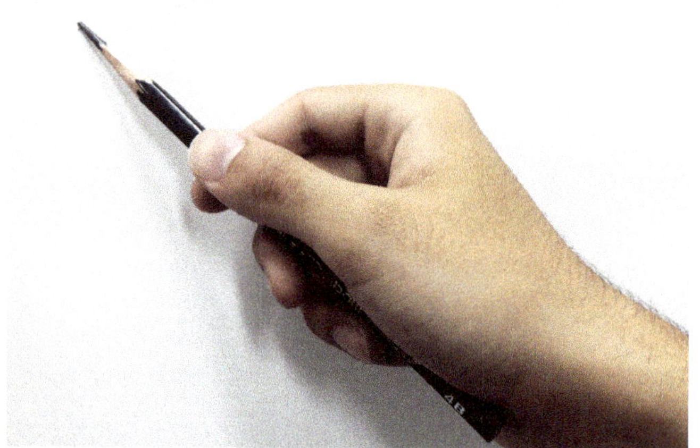

Use this position for even more control over your marks and in creating darks. Vary the length of your grip for a variation in the darkness of your marks; the shorter the grip, the darker the mark, and the longer the grip, the lighter the mark.

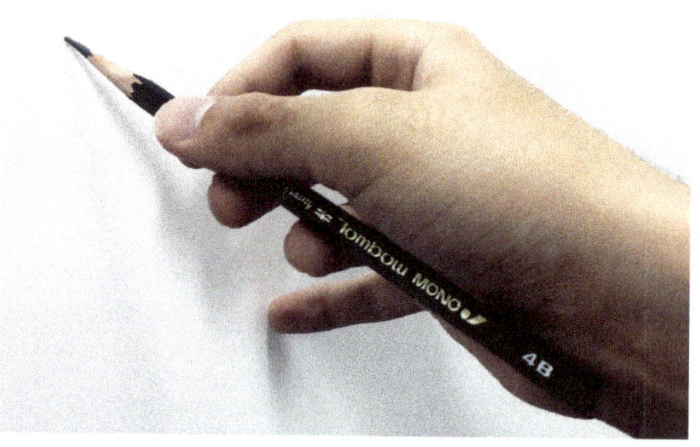

Hold the pencil close to the tip, leaving the tip of your pinky on the paper to create a tripod for more control over your marks and to avoid smudging your work. This position will allow you to create very fine, delicate lines and details.

Shading Techniques

Different values, whether shadows or highlights, will lift your subject off the two dimensions of your drawing surface, making it more three-dimensional and more realistic. Value is sometimes referred to as "tone," which is directly affected by the degree, direction, and quality of light upon your subject.

Hatching Exercise

Make all your marks in the same direction

1	2	3	4	5	6	7	8	9	10

Cross Hatching Exercise

Create two layers of hatching using marks in different directions

1	2	3	4	5	6	7	8	9	10

Blending Exercise

Shade with a light and rounded motion to minimize the appearance of any strokes

1	2	3	4	5	6	7	8	9	10

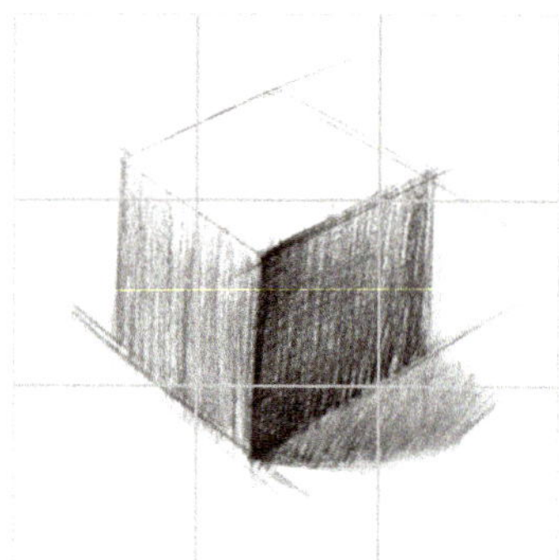
Keep base lines parallel to one another.

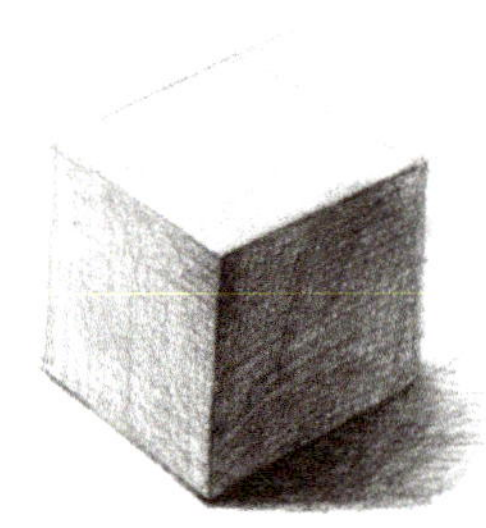
Begin to shade in the general areas of shadow by identifying the darker and lighter sides.

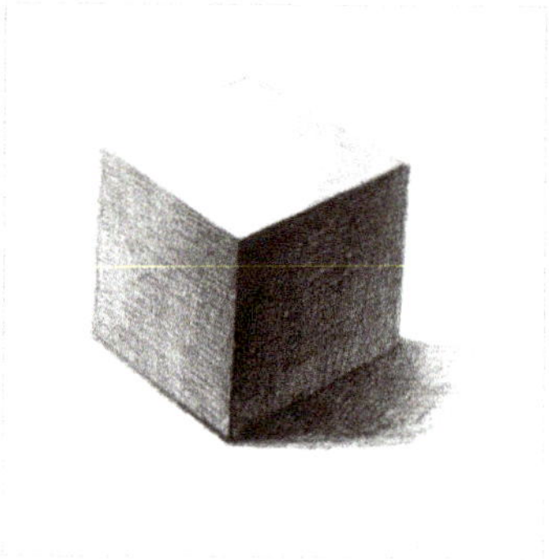

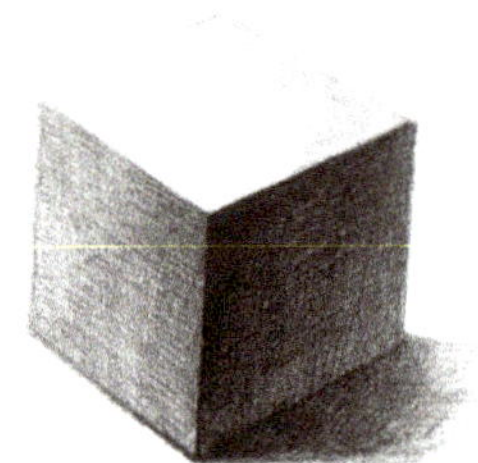
Even out the sides, develop the shadow, and erase unnecessary lines.

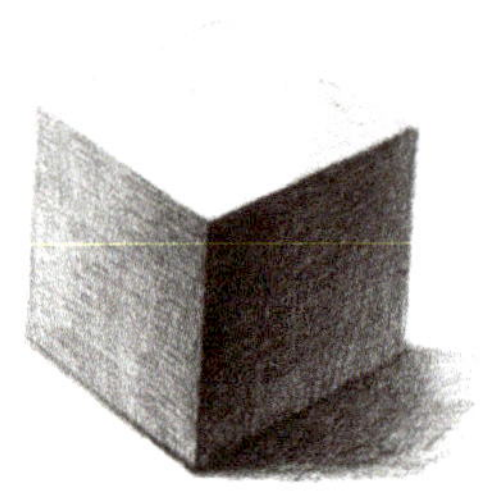
Continue to develop the shadows and clean up edges with an eraser.

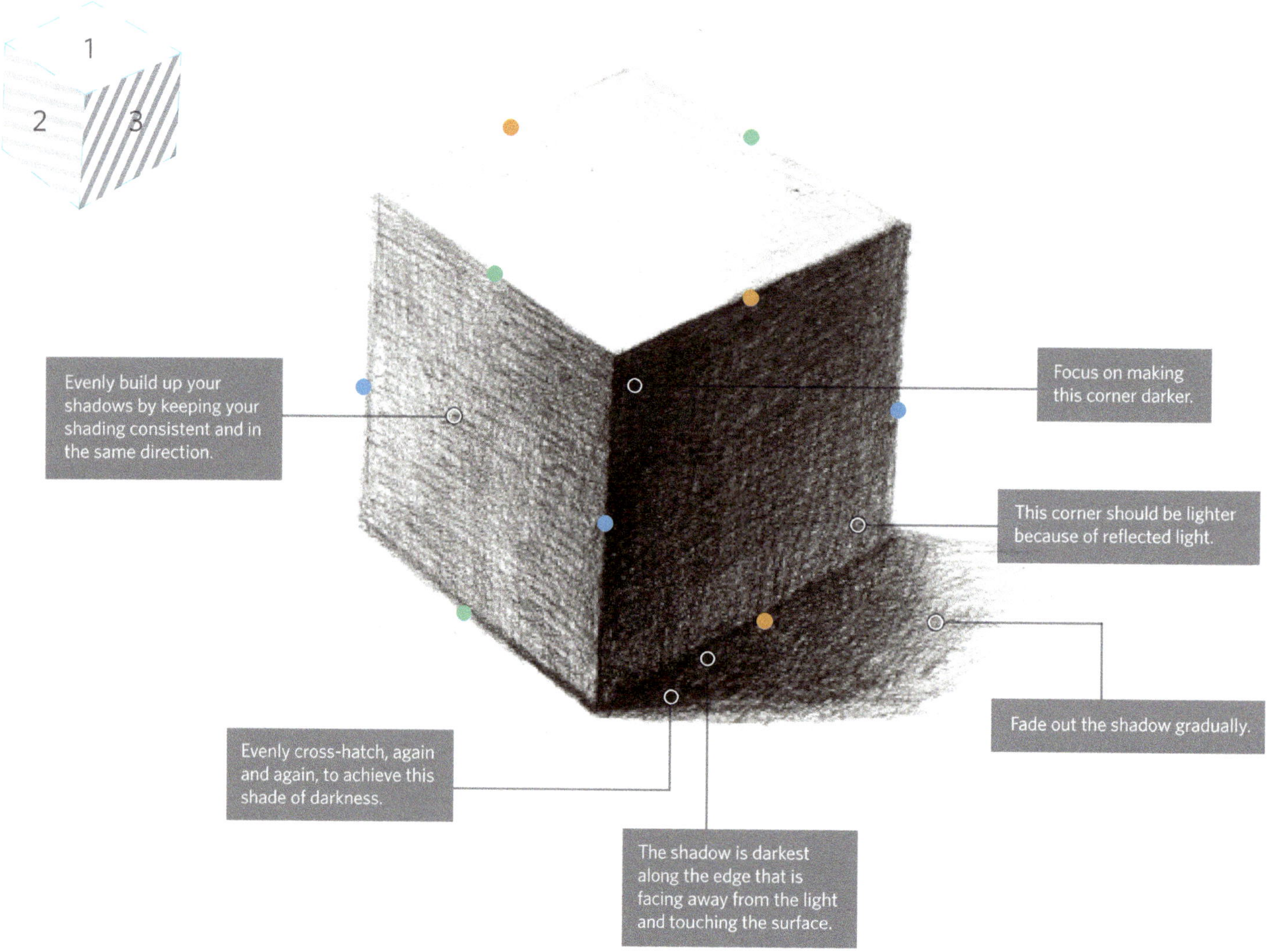

1

2 3

Evenly build up your shadows by keeping your shading consistent and in the same direction.

Focus on making this corner darker.

This corner should be lighter because of reflected light.

Fade out the shadow gradually.

Evenly cross-hatch, again and again, to achieve this shade of darkness.

The shadow is darkest along the edge that is facing away from the light and touching the surface.

KEY

- (green) Keep these lines parallel to one another.
- (orange) Keep these lines parallel to one another.
- (blue) Keep these lines parallel to the left and right edges of your paper.

Now try drawing the cube yourself.

This exercise will teach you to understand how shadows fall on different sides of an object. All objects have different sides since they are three-dimensional, and these sides will be different tones depending on how they interact with the light source. The sides facing away from the light source are darker; therefore, sides closer to the light soure are lighter.

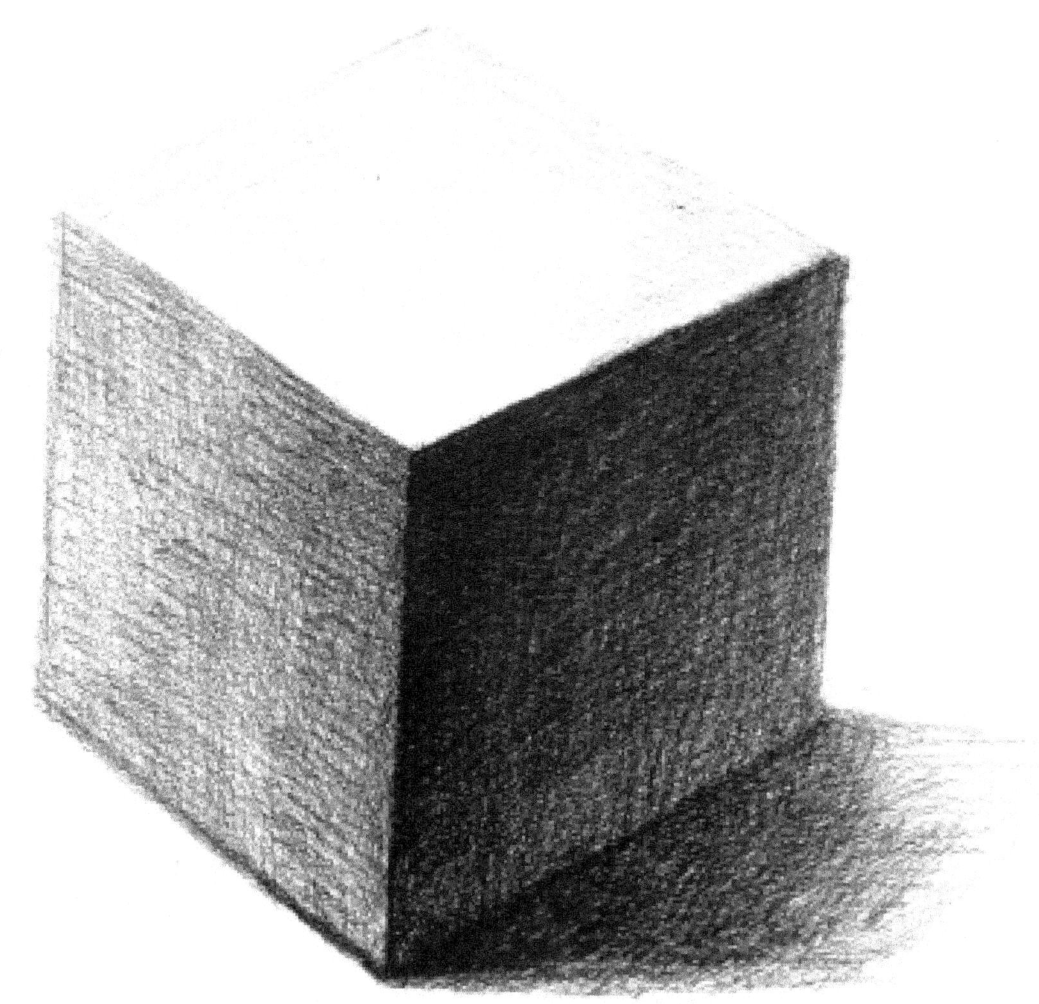

Now try drawing the cube using the reference picture without any grid lines.

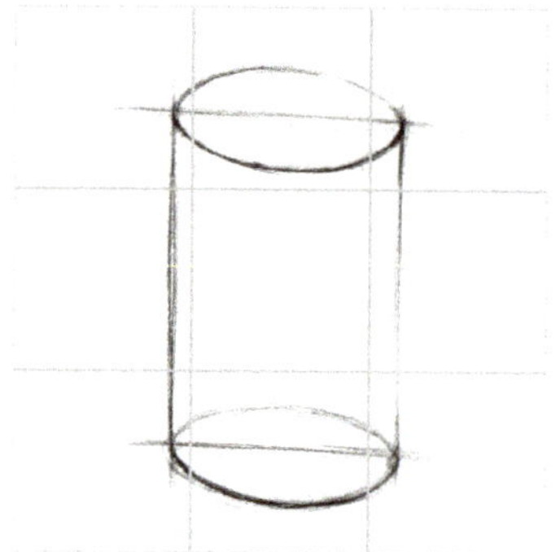

Sketch out the general shape of the cylinder. Keep these lines parallel to one another.

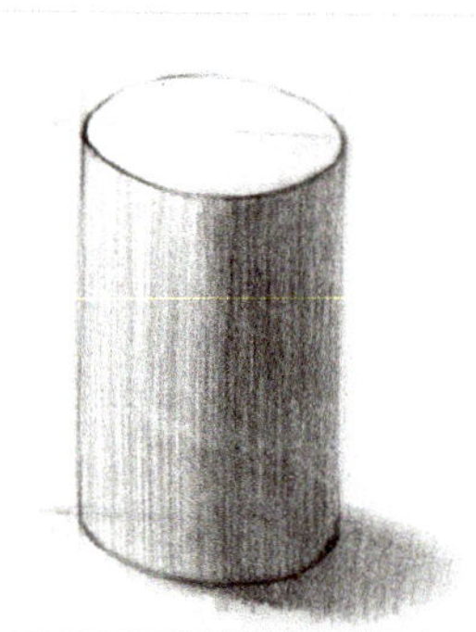

Begin to shade in the general tones by shading in where the darker shadow meets the lighter shadow.

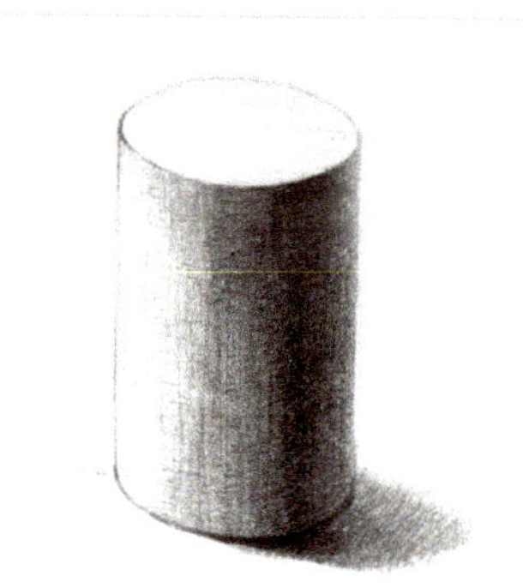

Clean up unnecessary lines as you continue to recognize the darks, lights, and middle tones.

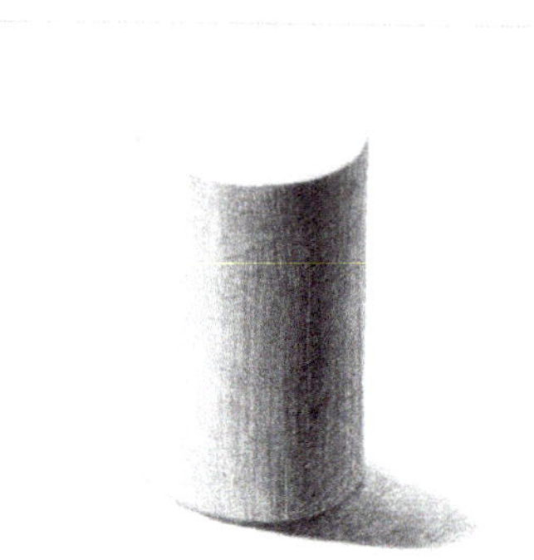

Fully develop your drawing using the complete range of tones.

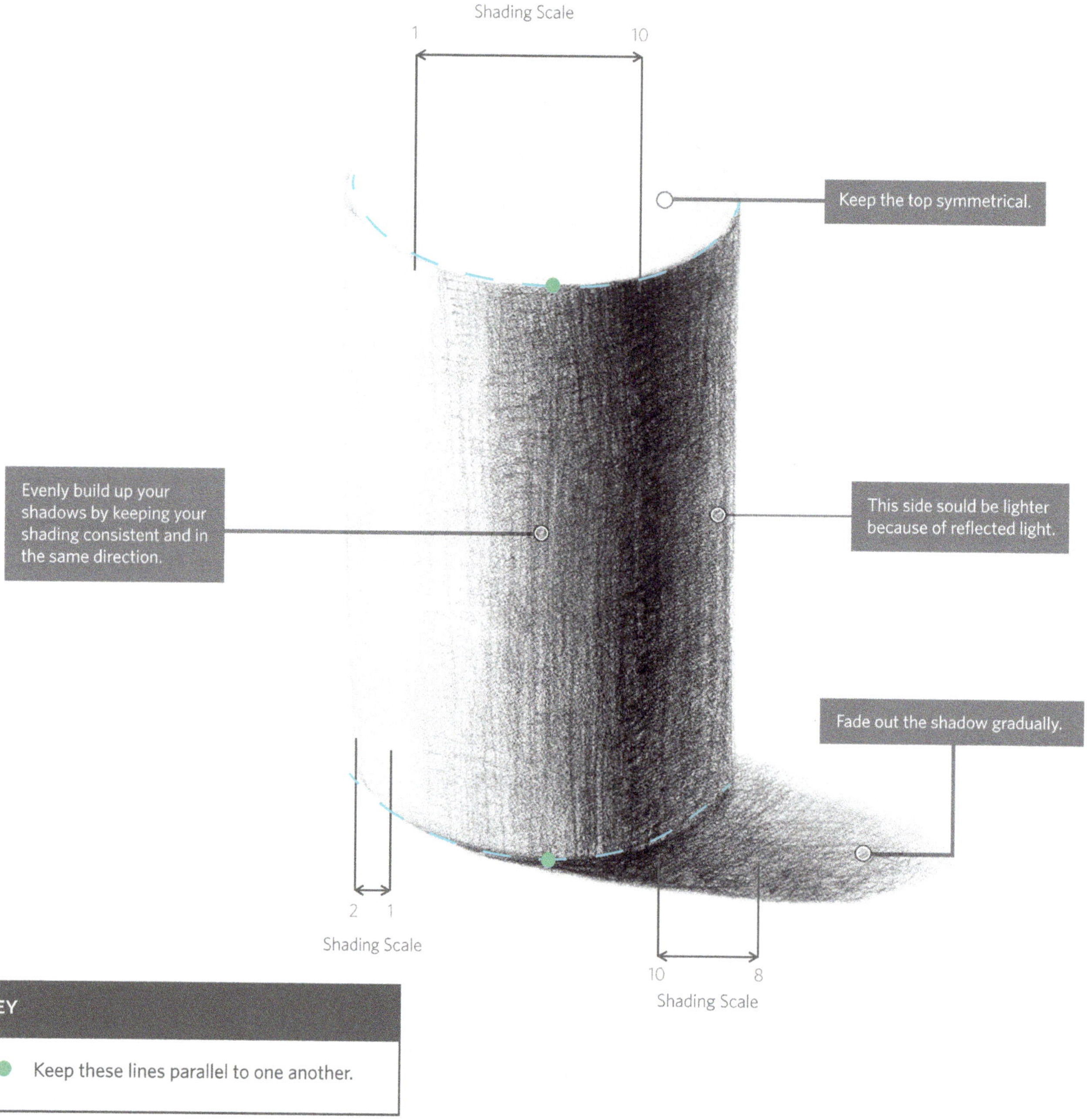

Shading Scale

1 10

Keep the top symmetrical.

Evenly build up your shadows by keeping your shading consistent and in the same direction.

This side sould be lighter because of reflected light.

Fade out the shadow gradually.

2 1

Shading Scale

10 8

Shading Scale

KEY

● Keep these lines parallel to one another.

Now try drawing the cylinder yourself.

Objects with a smooth, continuous surface are harder to draw than objects with flat sides and rigid corners, such as cubes. For cylinders, render the tones evenly from darkest to lightest to suggest a round shape. Remember to round out the bottom edge of the cylinder to make the roundness more believable.

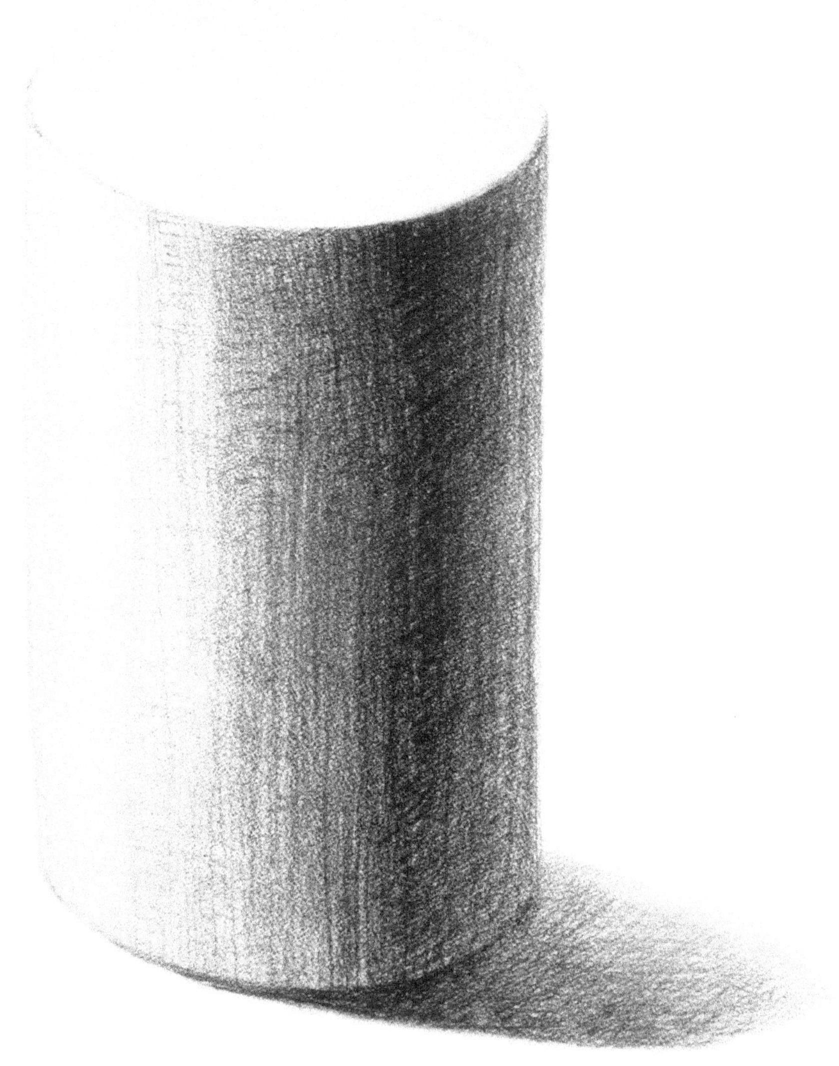

Now try drawing the cylinder using the reference picture without any grid lines.

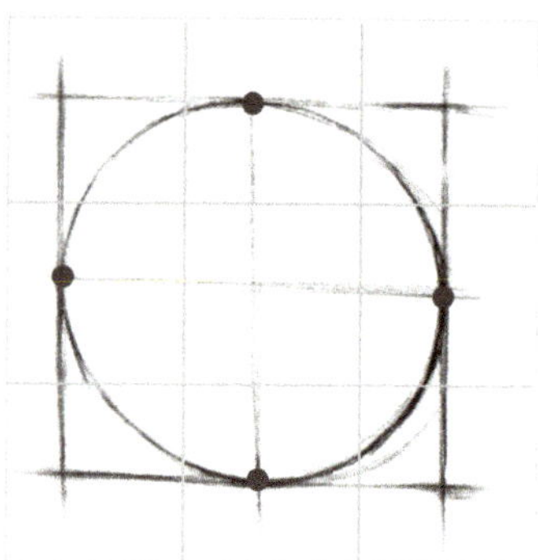
First sketch out a perfect square. Then use the dots to guide you to draw a circle.

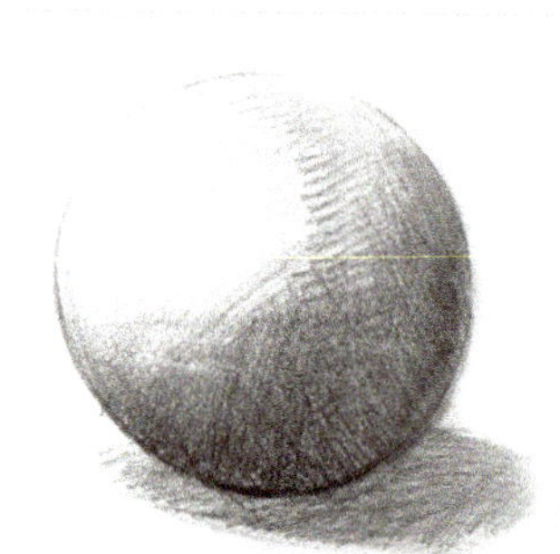
Shade in the general areas of the shadows.

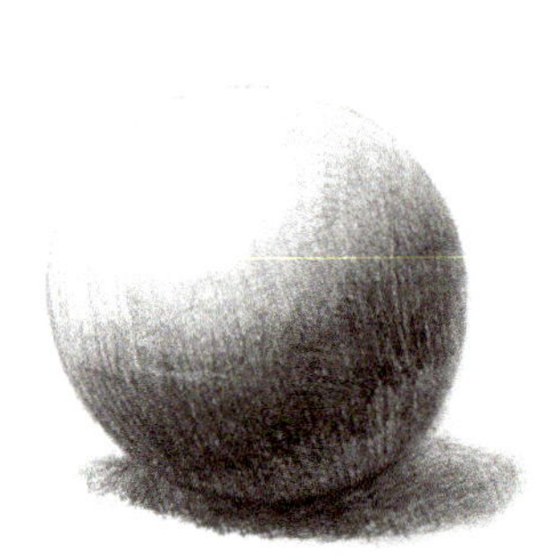
Develop your shadows by defining where the darkest areas of the shadows are.

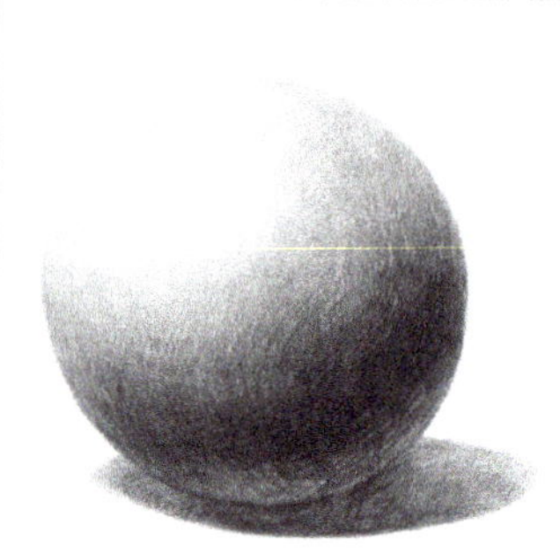
Continue adding in the full range of tones to make your sphere more three-dimentional.

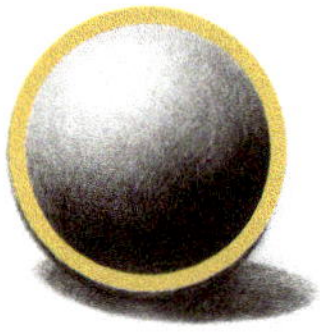

Focus on capturing the circular contour of the sphere first.

Notice how almost no contrast exists between the edge of the sphere and the white of the paper.

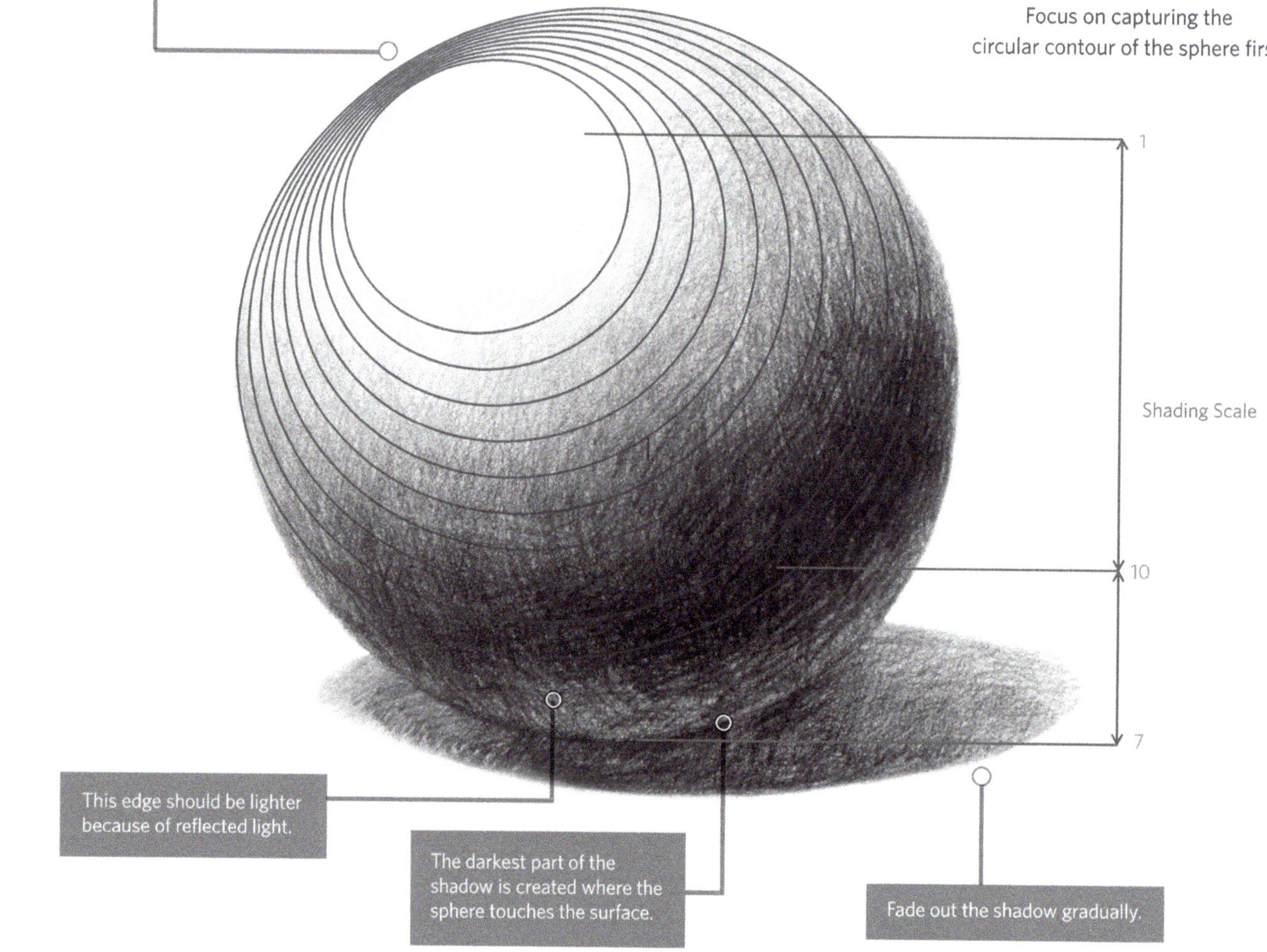

1

Shading Scale

10

7

This edge should be lighter because of reflected light.

The darkest part of the shadow is created where the sphere touches the surface.

Fade out the shadow gradually.

Now try drawing the cylinder yourself.

Drawing a sphere is like drawing a cylinder, but perfectly round and smooth on all sides. Try drawing in a circular motion to further create the illusion of a rounded sphere. For the brighest parts of the sphere, remember that the eraser is also another form of mark-making. Use the eraser to create a smooth bright highlight.

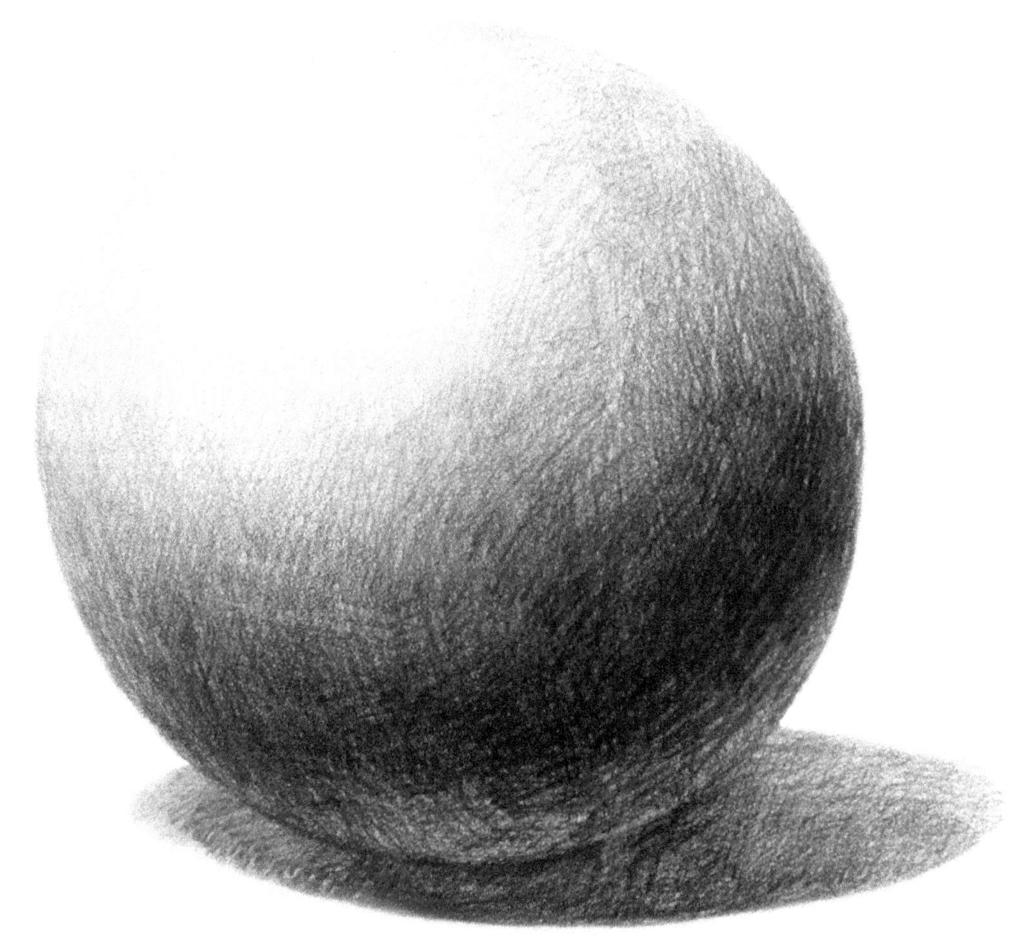

Now try drawing the sphere using the reference picture without any grid lines.

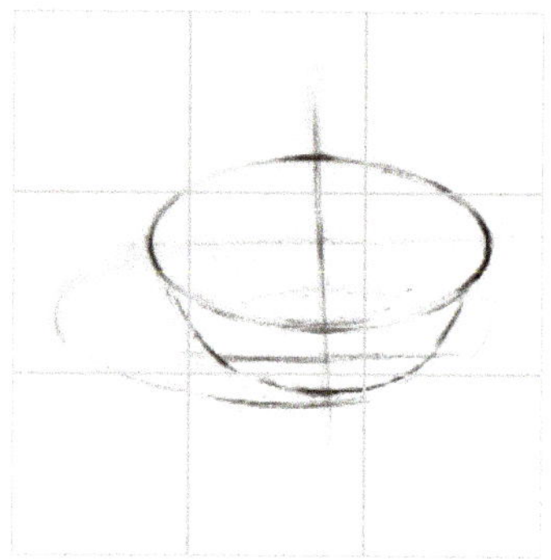
Sketch out the general shape of the bowl. Use lines to help you in drawing the bowl's lip, remember, it's an ellipse.

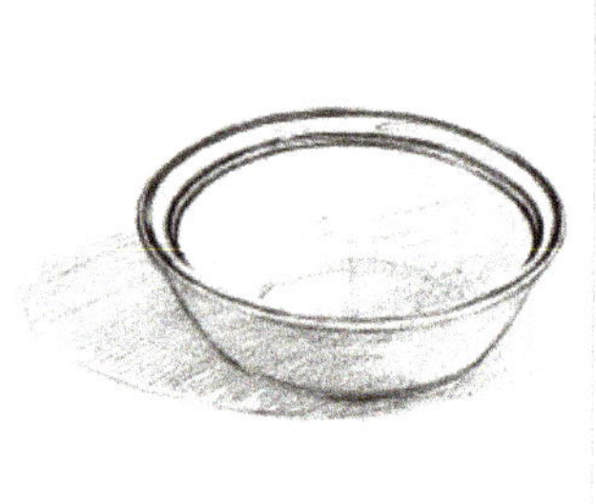
Begin to add in the general areas of shadow.

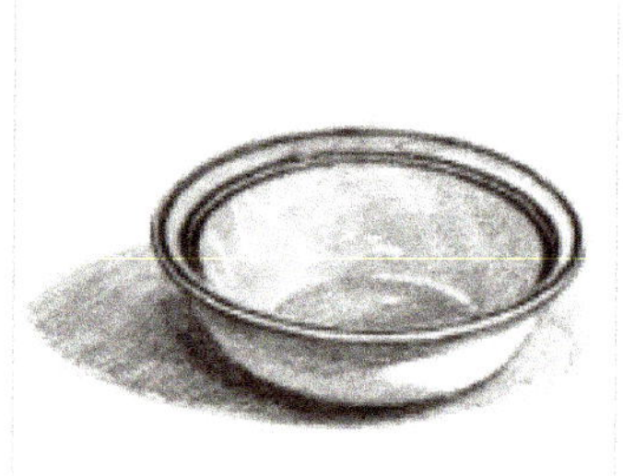
Continue to develop the darks, lights, and middle tones.

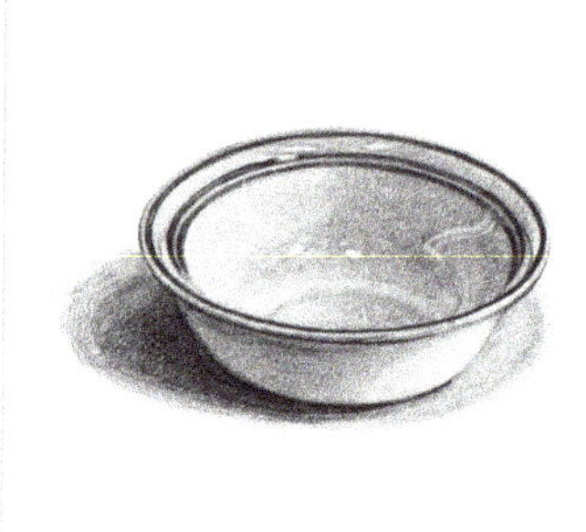
Use the entire range of tones to completely develop your drawing.

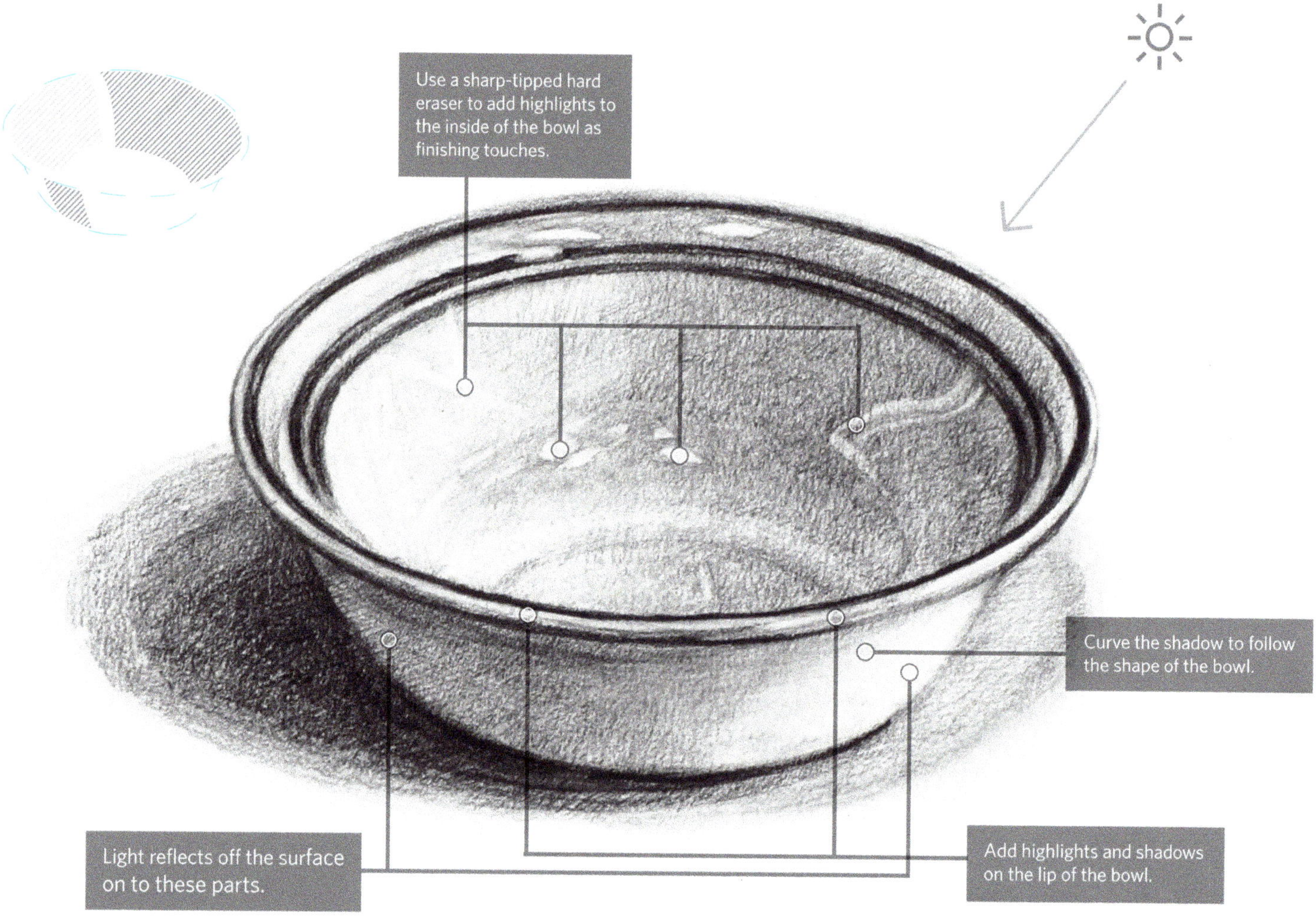

Use a sharp-tipped hard eraser to add highlights to the inside of the bowl as finishing touches.

Curve the shadow to follow the shape of the bowl.

Light reflects off the surface on to these parts.

Add highlights and shadows on the lip of the bowl.

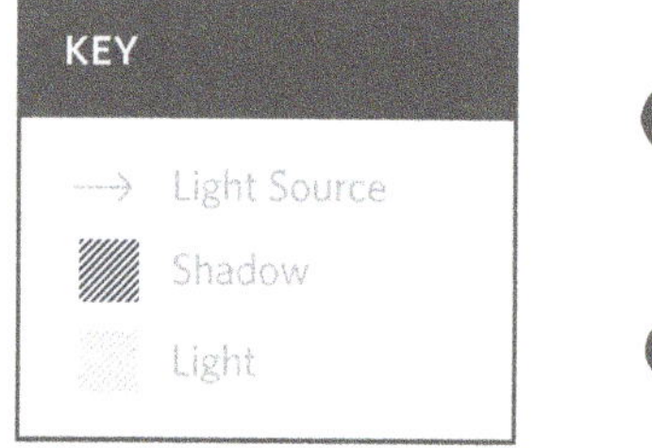

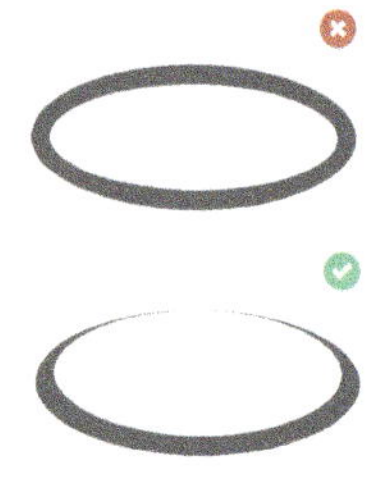

Now try drawing the bowl yourself.

Drawing a bowl is like drawing a cylinder with one end rounded in. Don't be intimidated by its shiny surface, instead focus on the general areas of shadow before going into the details. When drawing reflective surfaces, it's important to use the sharp edge of an eraser to create light reflections to create the illusion of a shiny surface.

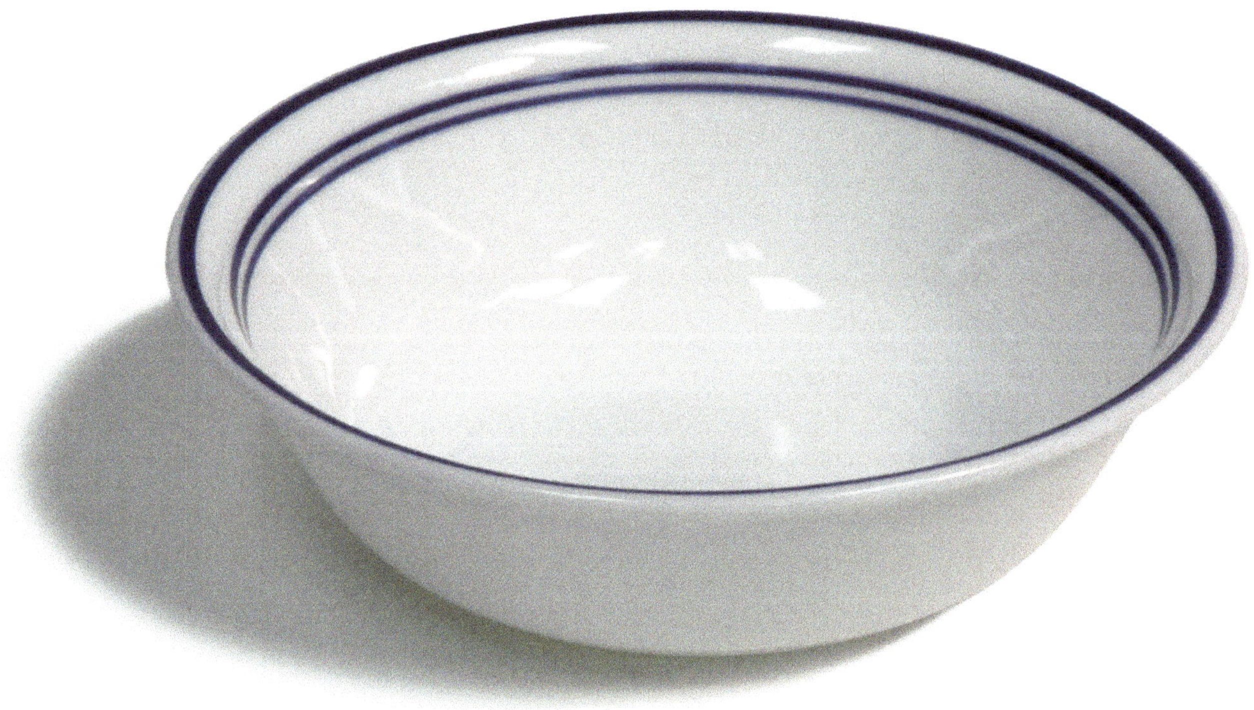

Now try drawing the bowl using the reference picture without any grid lines.

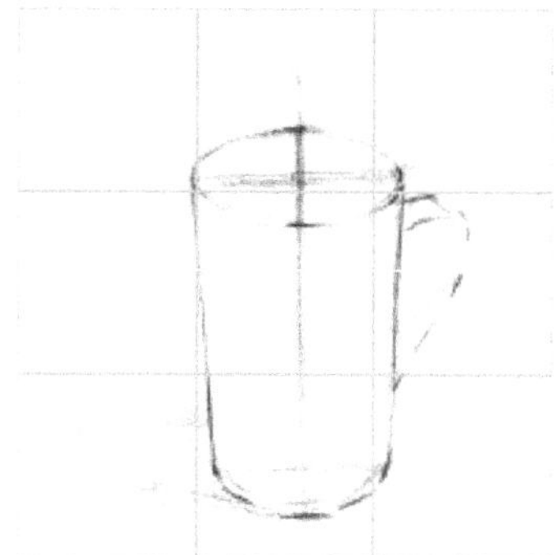

Sketch the general shape of the cup, it's like combining a cylinder with a handle.

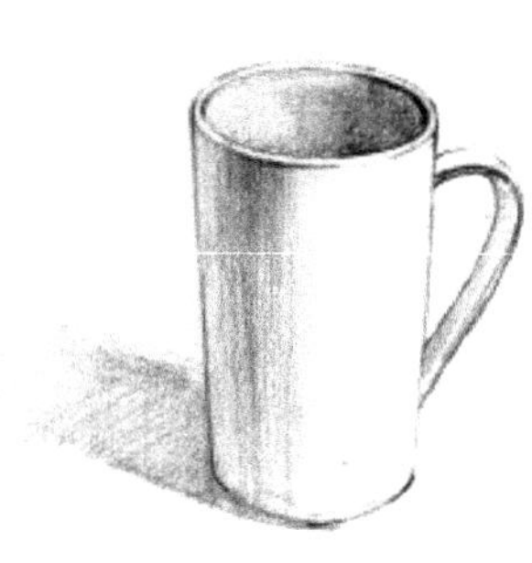

Identify the light source and shade in the general areas of shadow accordingly.

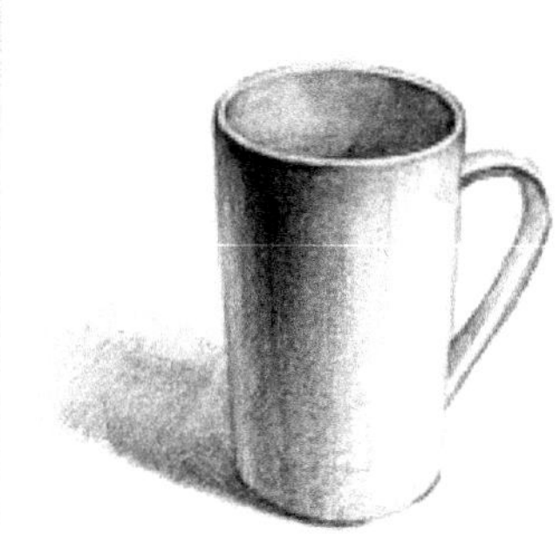

Continue to identify the darks, lights, and middle tones.

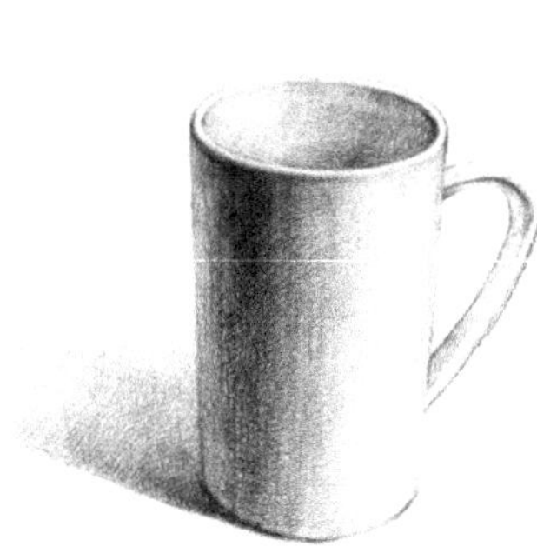

Use the entire range of tones to completely develop your drawing.

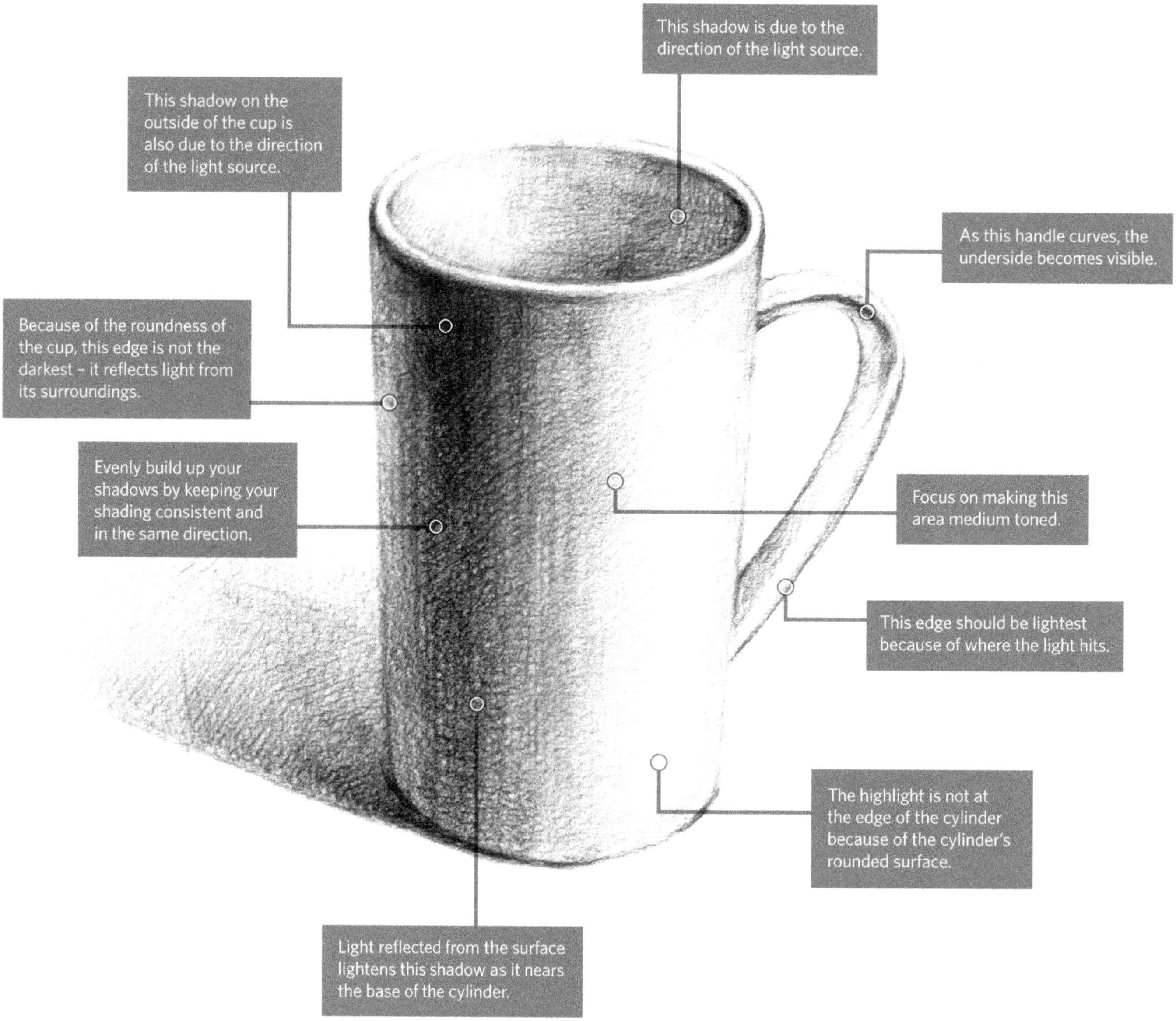

This shadow is due to the direction of the light source.

This shadow on the outside of the cup is also due to the direction of the light source.

As this handle curves, the underside becomes visible.

Because of the roundness of the cup, this edge is not the darkest – it reflects light from its surroundings.

Evenly build up your shadows by keeping your shading consistent and in the same direction.

Focus on making this area medium toned.

This edge should be lightest because of where the light hits.

The highlight is not at the edge of the cylinder because of the cylinder's rounded surface.

Light reflected from the surface lightens this shadow as it nears the base of the cylinder.

Now try drawing the cup yourself.

The most important thing to remember when drawing any cup is that the shadows casted on the outside of the cup fall on the opposite side inside of the cup.

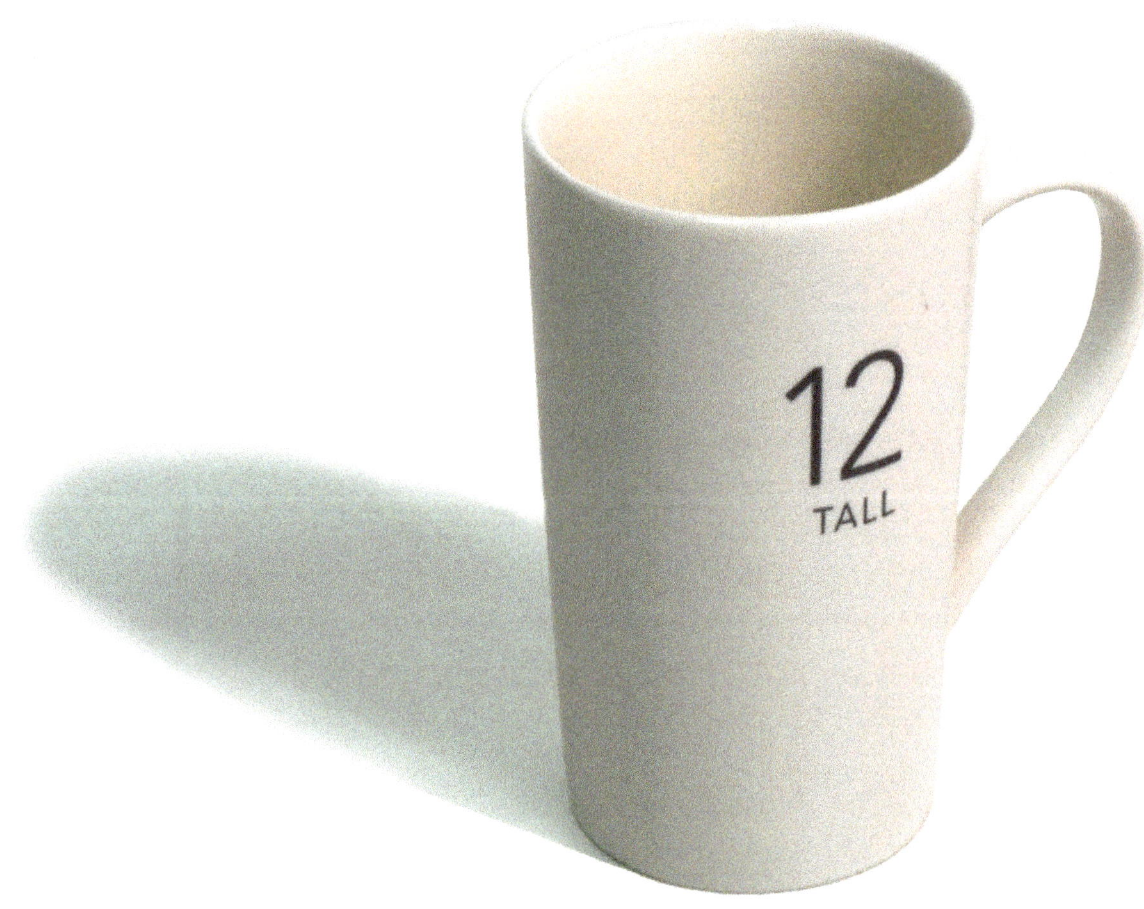

Now try drawing the cup using the reference picture without any grid lines.

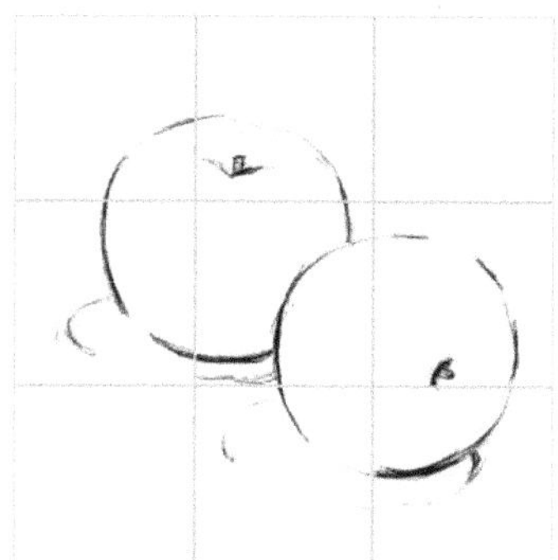
Sketch the general composition and shadows of the apples.

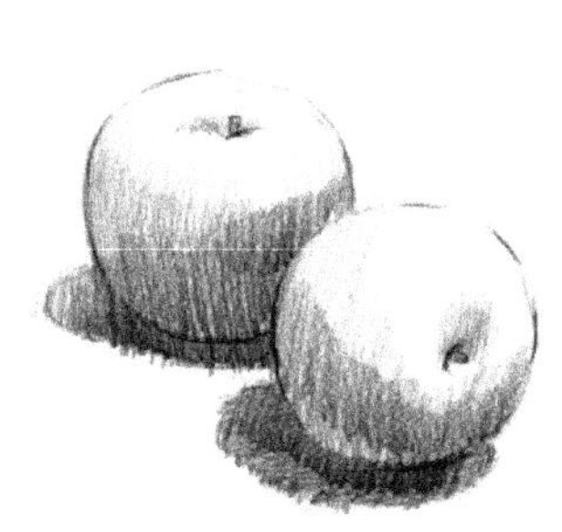
Identify the direction of the light source and shade in the general areas of shadow accordingly.

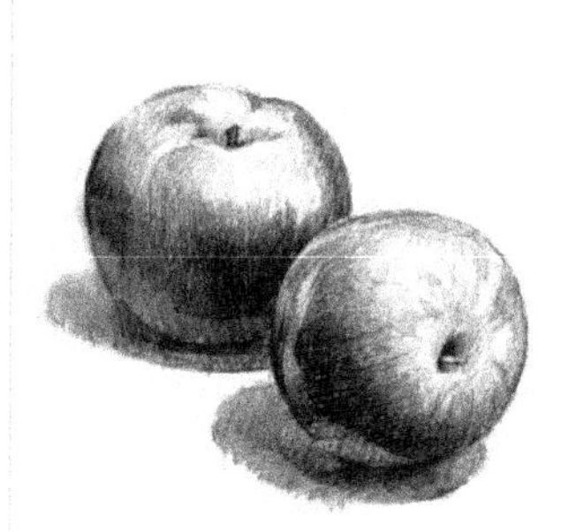
Continue to identify the darks, lights, and middle tones.

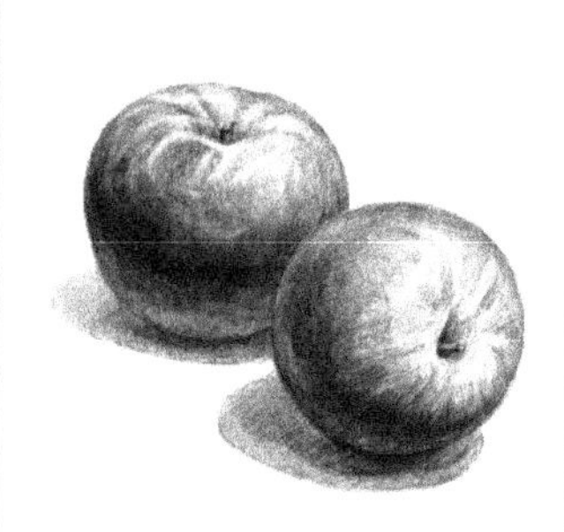
Make sure to use the entire range of tones to fully develop your drawing.

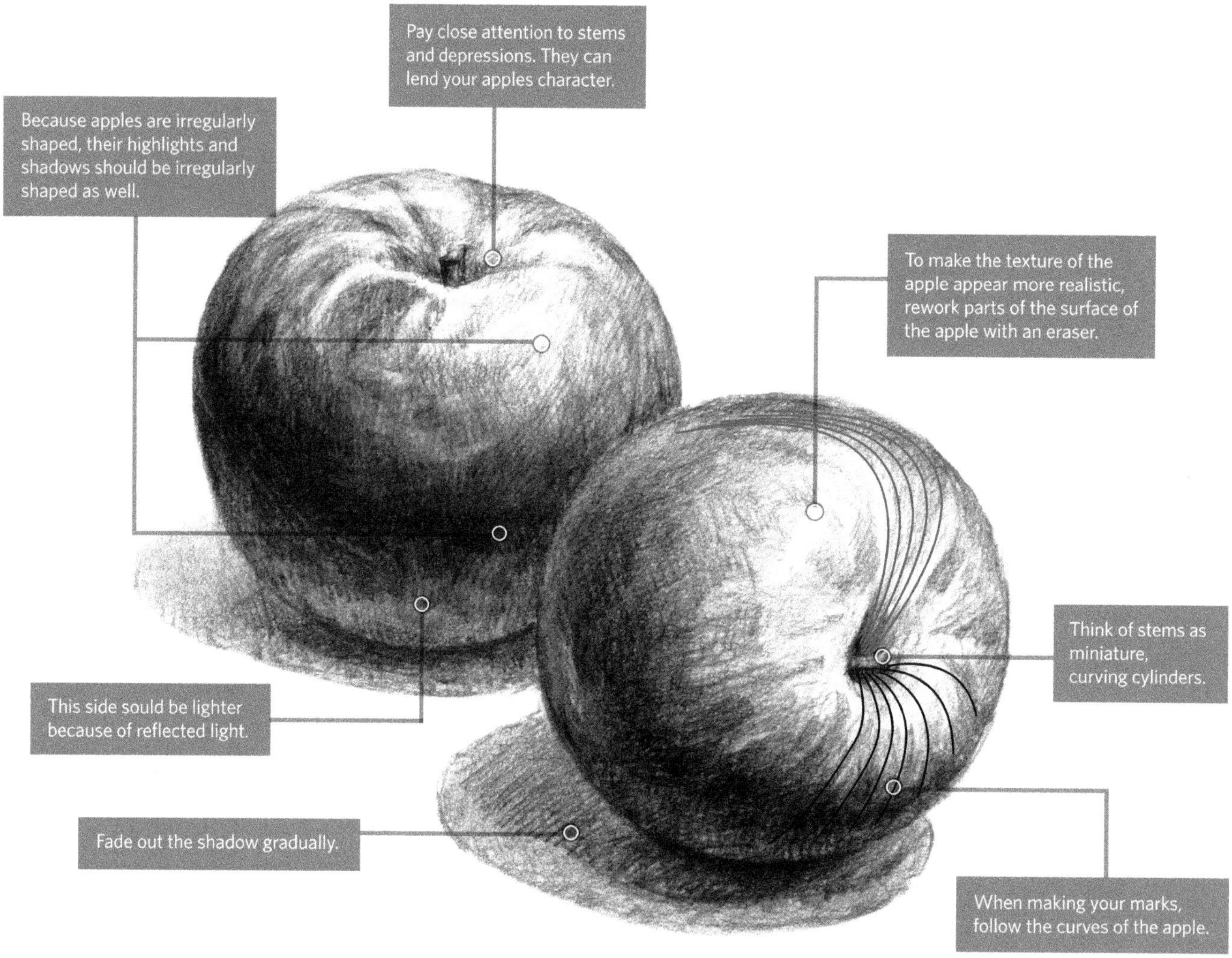

Pay close attention to stems and depressions. They can lend your apples character.

Because apples are irregularly shaped, their highlights and shadows should be irregularly shaped as well.

To make the texture of the apple appear more realistic, rework parts of the surface of the apple with an eraser.

Think of stems as miniature, curving cylinders.

This side sould be lighter because of reflected light.

Fade out the shadow gradually.

When making your marks, follow the curves of the apple.

Now try drawing the apple yourself.

These apples are a realistic approach to the shapes we've been practicing in previous exercises. Geometrically, these apples are irregular spheres with a depression where a curved cylinder comes out. Capture the irregularities in shape and color to make your apples more realistic.

Breaking down objects into simple geometric forms and working gradually from general to detailed is a great way of making challenging still life drawings easier.

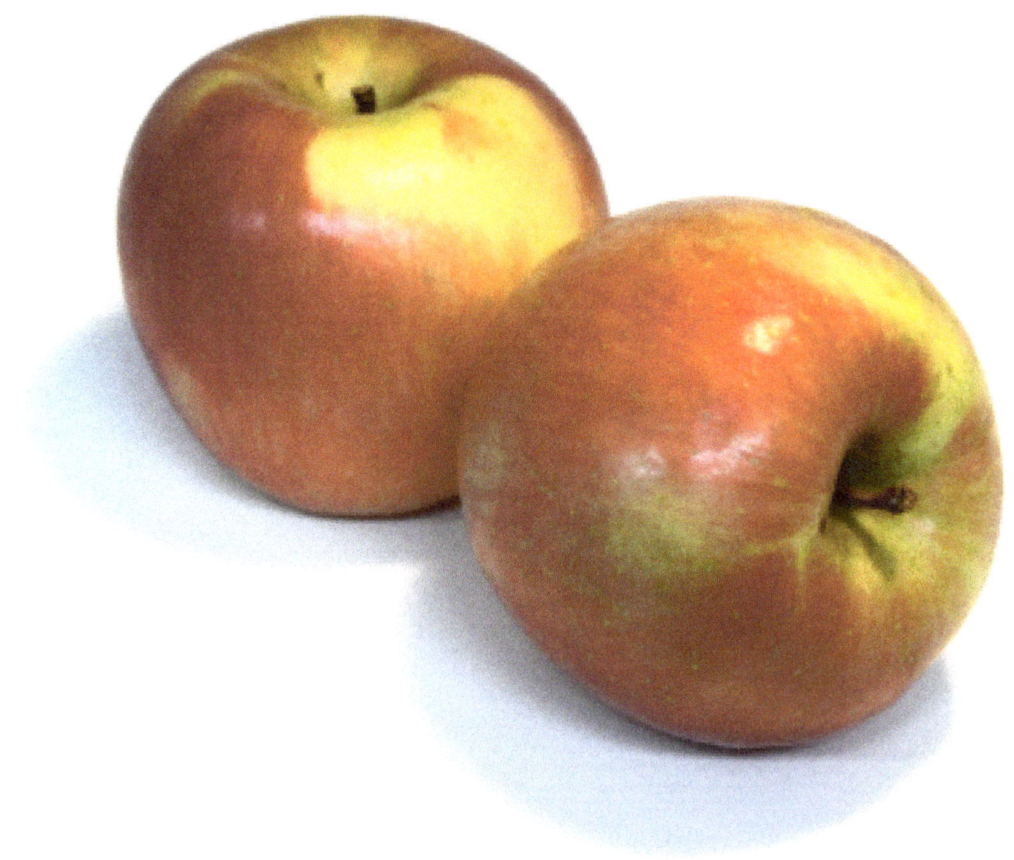

Now try drawing the apple using the reference picture without any grid lines.

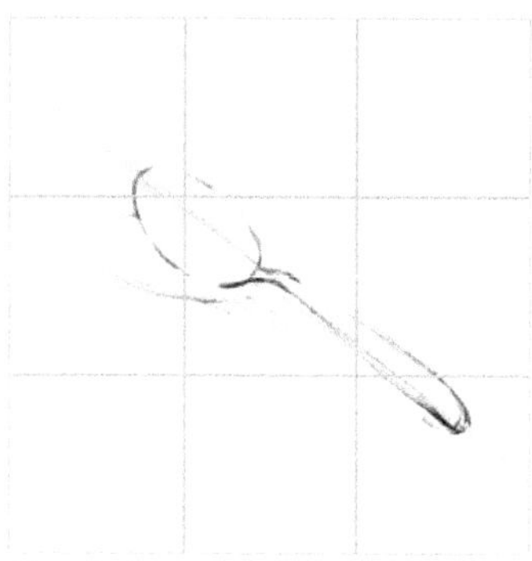

Sketch the general shape of the spoon, using a center line to help you with symmetry.

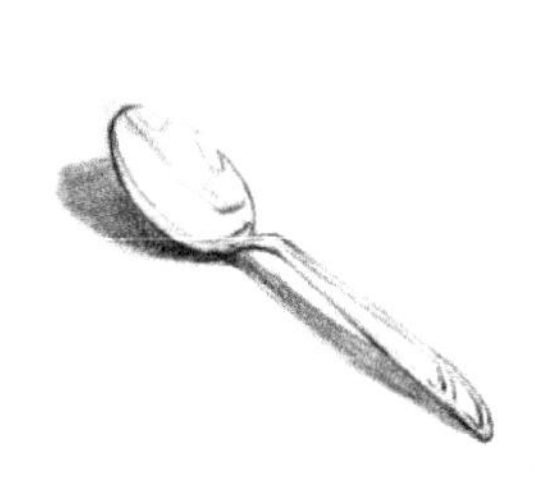

Identify the direction of the light source and shade in the general areas of shadow accordingly.

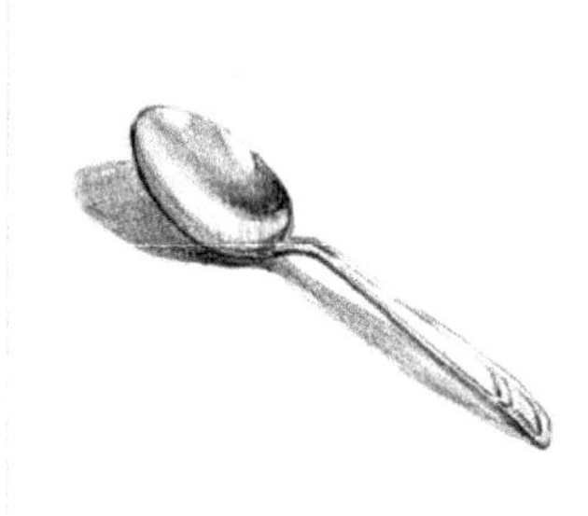

Continue to identify the darks, lights, and middle tones.

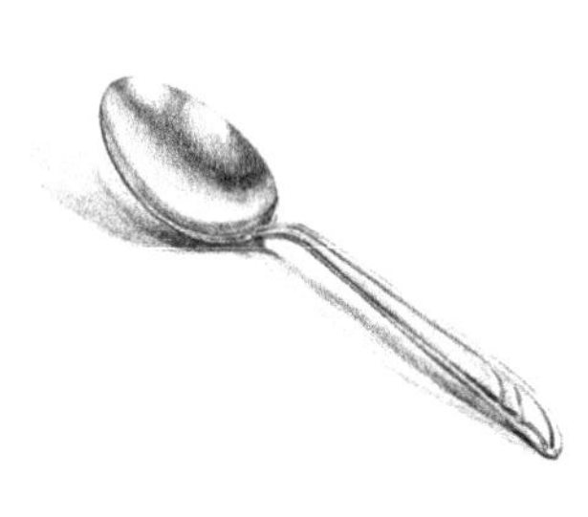

Make sure to use the entire range of tones to fully develop your drawing.

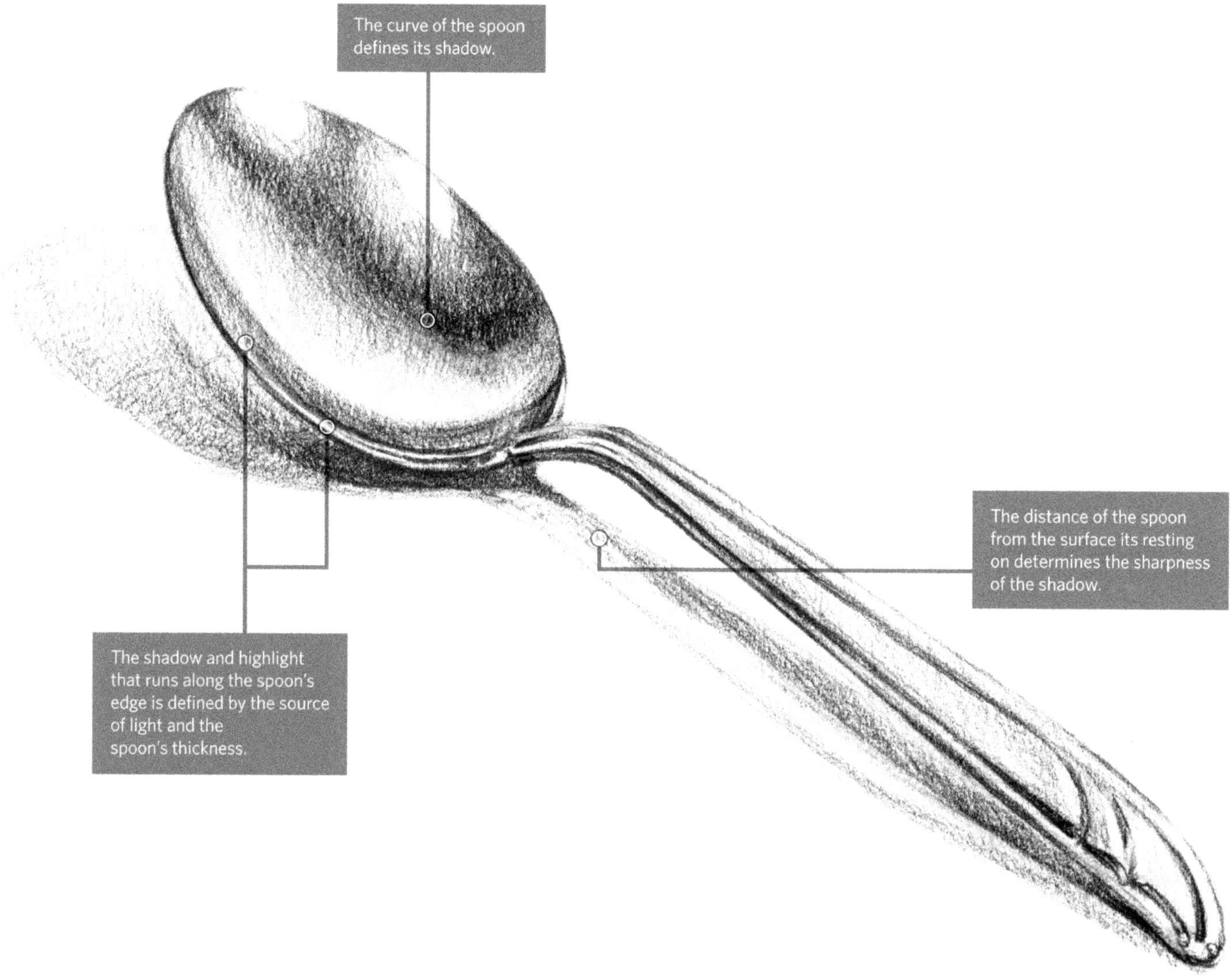

The curve of the spoon defines its shadow.

The distance of the spoon from the surface its resting on determines the sharpness of the shadow.

The shadow and highlight that runs along the spoon's edge is defined by the source of light and the spoon's thickness.

Now try drawing the spoon yourself.

Spoons can be challenging objects to draw because of their varying thicknesses, individual engravings, and also their metallic and curved reflections. Keep in mind to work gradually from general to specific in order to maintain the illusion of a curved spoon, otherwise your spoon may appear oddly bent. The more details you can capture, the more realistic the spoon you're rendering in pencil will become.

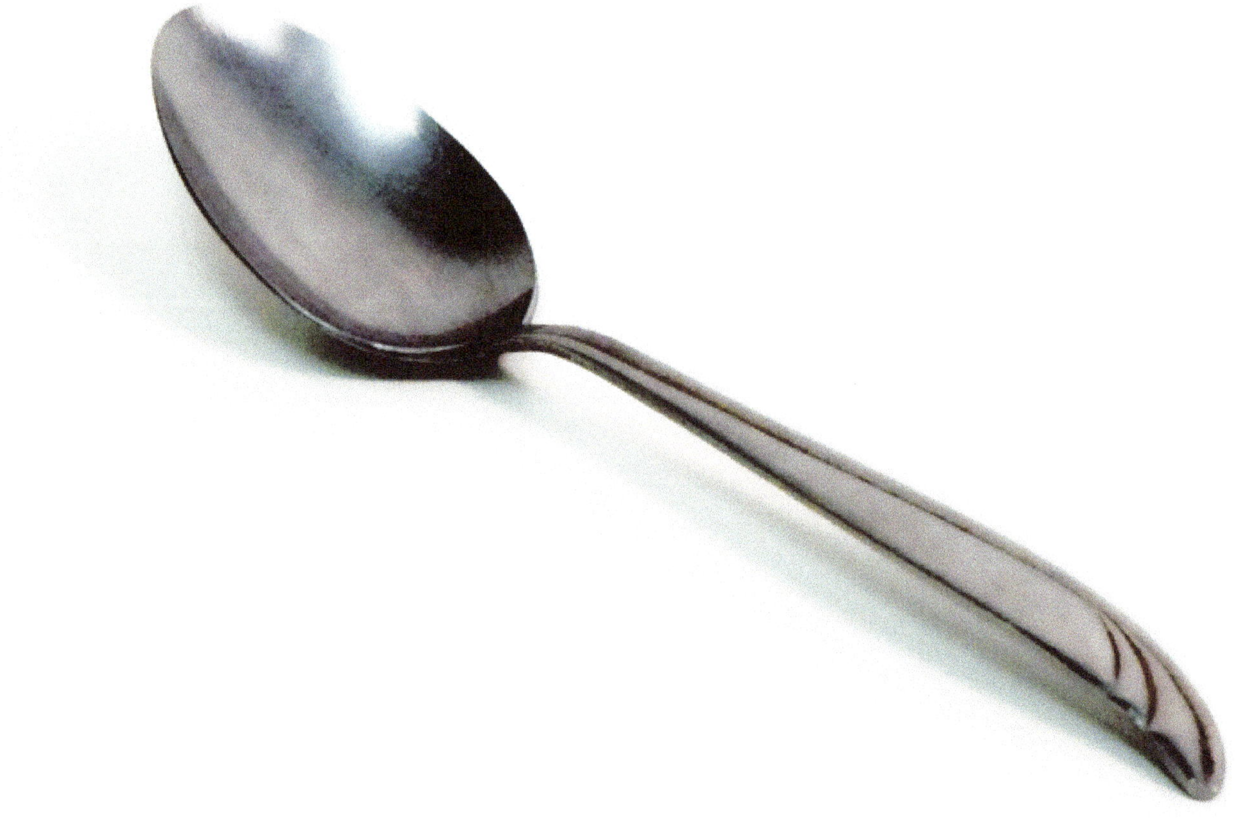

Now try drawing the spoon using the reference picture without any grid lines.

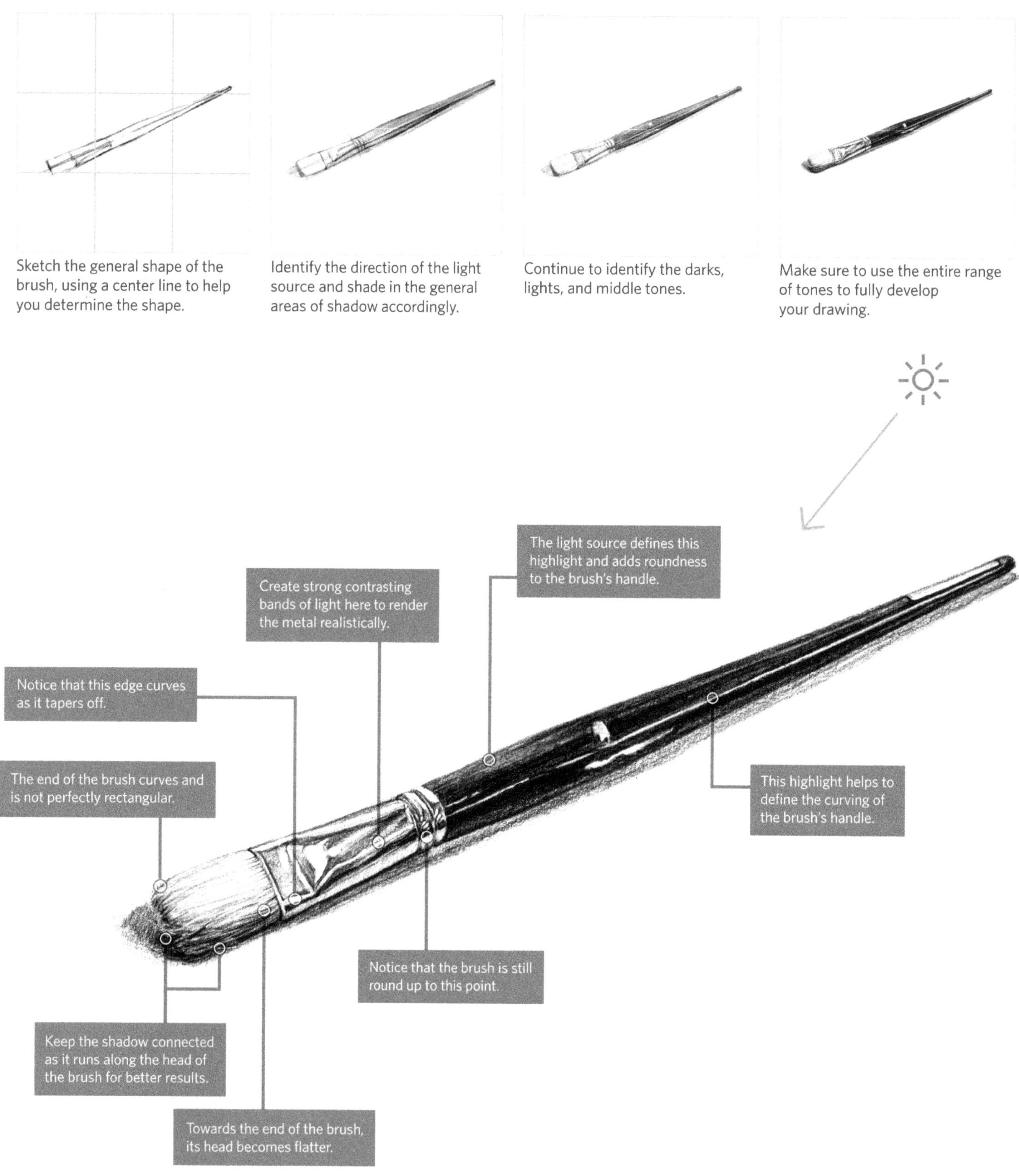
Sketch the general shape of the brush, using a center line to help you determine the shape.
Identify the direction of the light source and shade in the general areas of shadow accordingly.
Continue to identify the darks, lights, and middle tones.
Make sure to use the entire range of tones to fully develop your drawing.
The light source defines this highlight and adds roundness to the brush's handle.
Create strong contrasting bands of light here to render the metal realistically.
Notice that this edge curves as it tapers off.
The end of the brush curves and is not perfectly rectangular.
This highlight helps to define the curving of the brush's handle.
Notice that the brush is still round up to this point.
Keep the shadow connected as it runs along the head of the brush for better results.
Towards the end of the brush, its head becomes flatter.

Now try drawing the small brush yourself.

The small brush combines many different techniques and textures, including hair, wood, and metal. Keep in mind the previous exercises that helped you render volume. Notice where the object changes in shape and texture to create the same illusion when drawing.

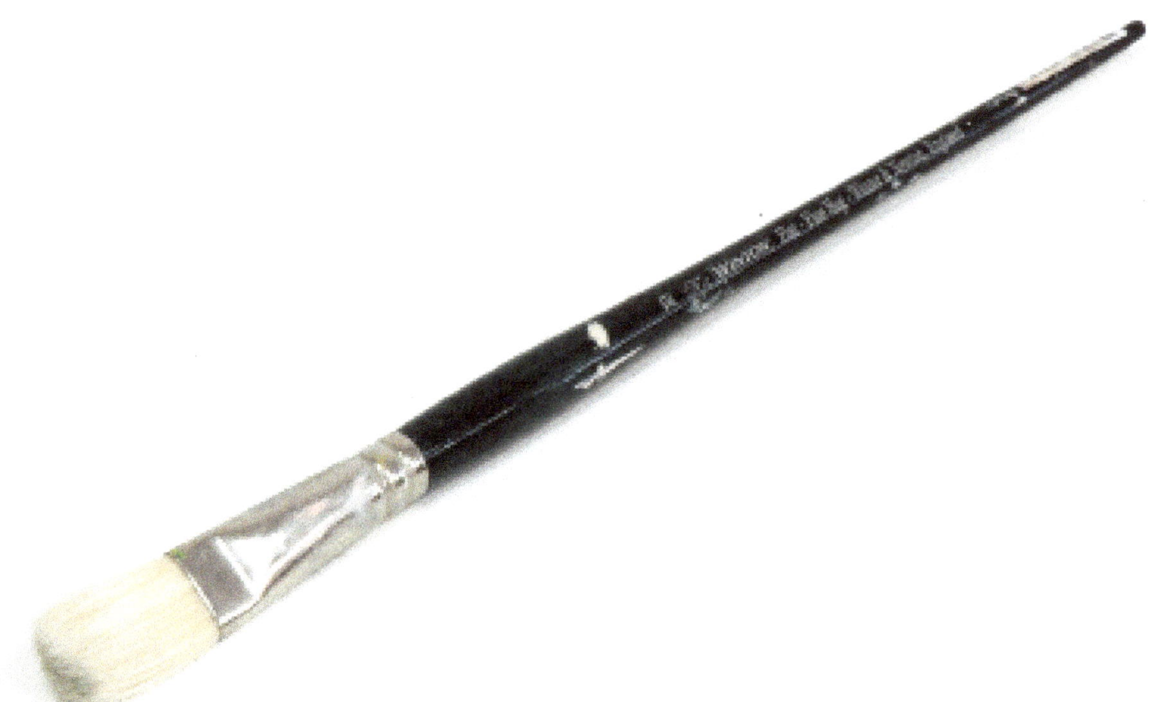

Now try drawing the small brush using the reference picture without any grid lines.

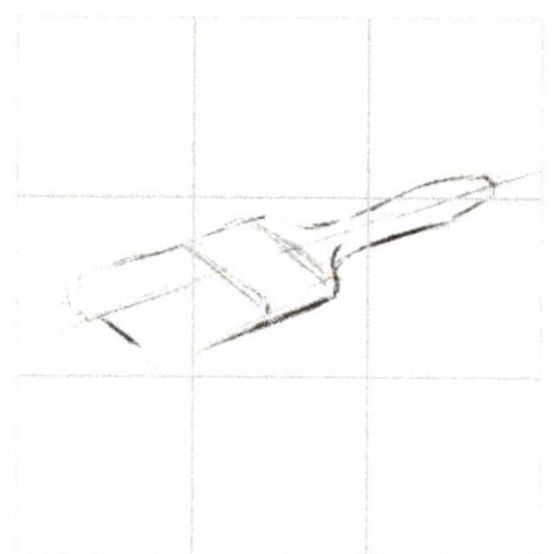

Sketch the general shape of the brush, using a center line to help you determine the shape.

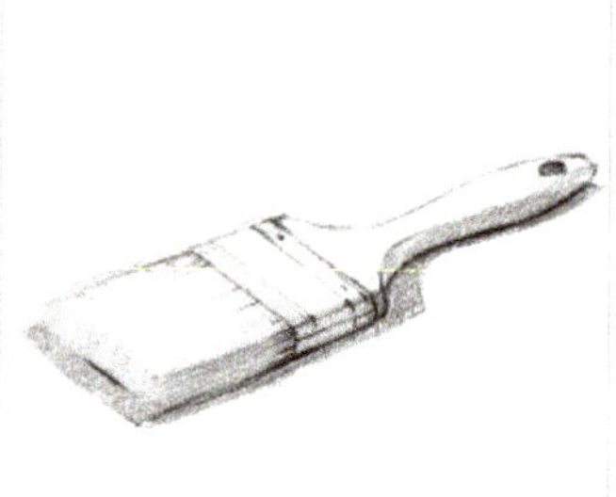

Identify the direction of the light source and shade in the general areas of shadow accordingly.

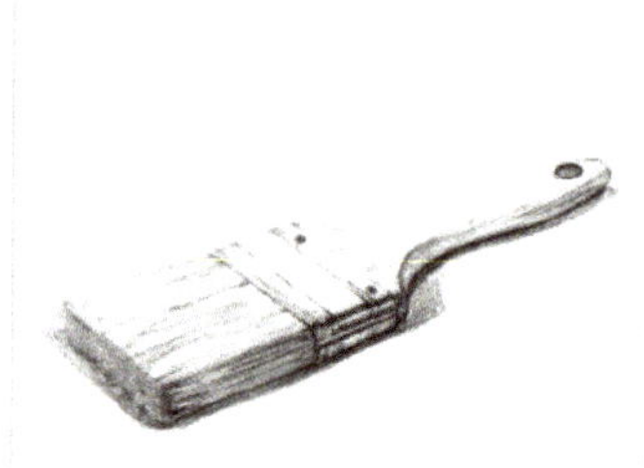

Continue to identify the darks, lights, and middle tones.

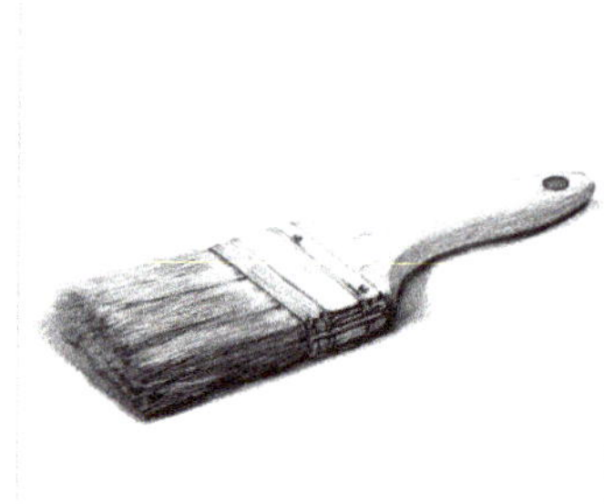

Make sure to use the entire range of tones to fully develop your drawing.

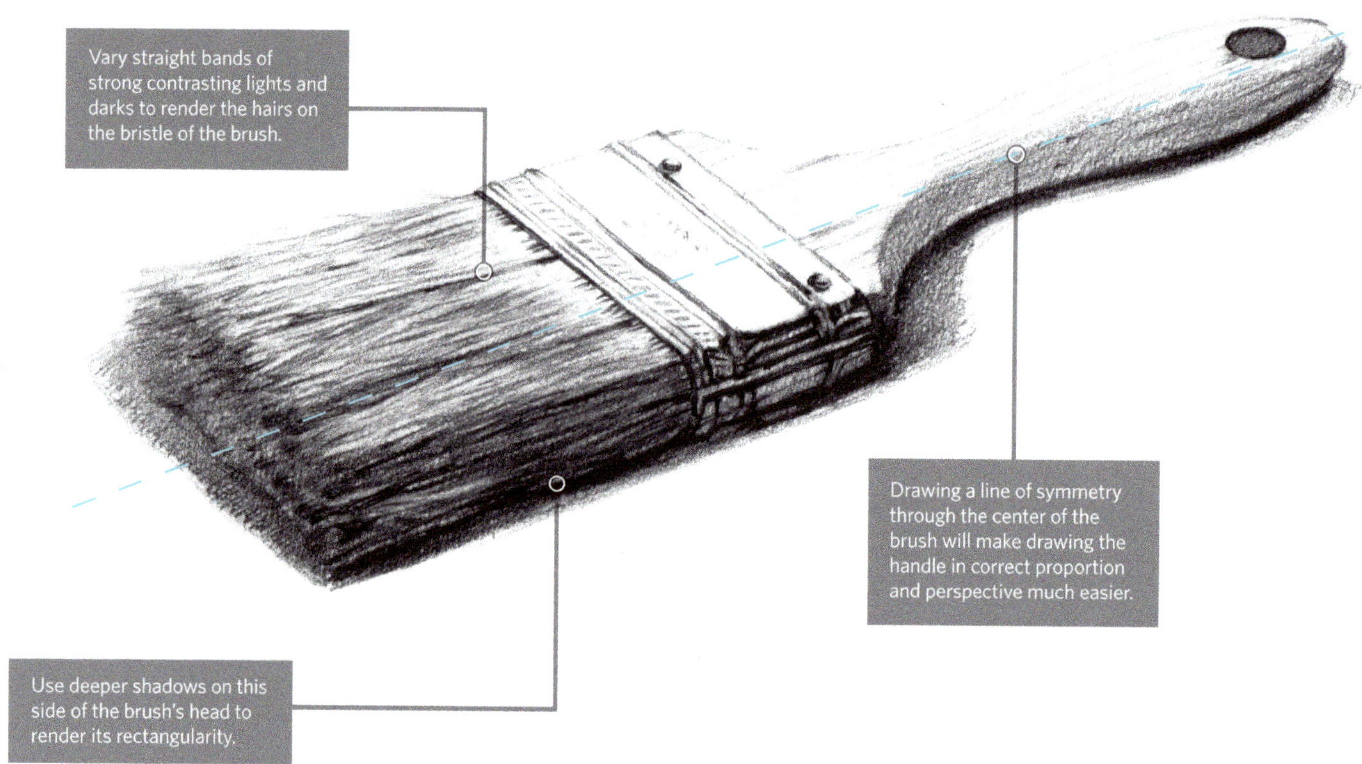

Now try drawing the large brush yourself.

Like the small brush, the large brush is an opportunity for you to practice the techniques you have been practicing, especially to further practice rendering hair, metal, and wood grain.

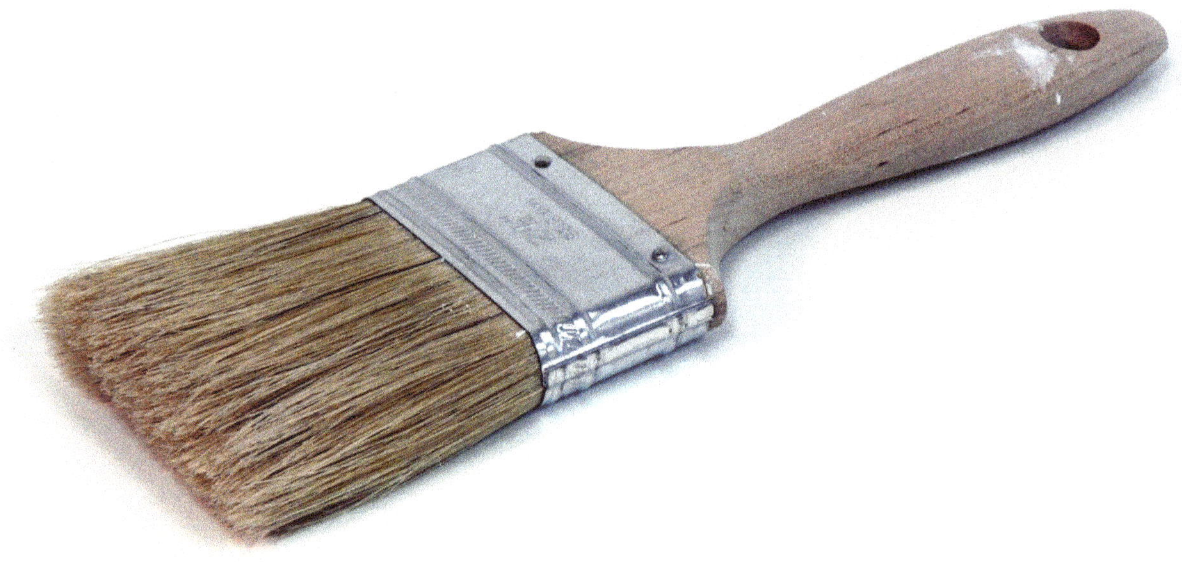

Now try drawing the large brush using the reference picture without any grid lines.

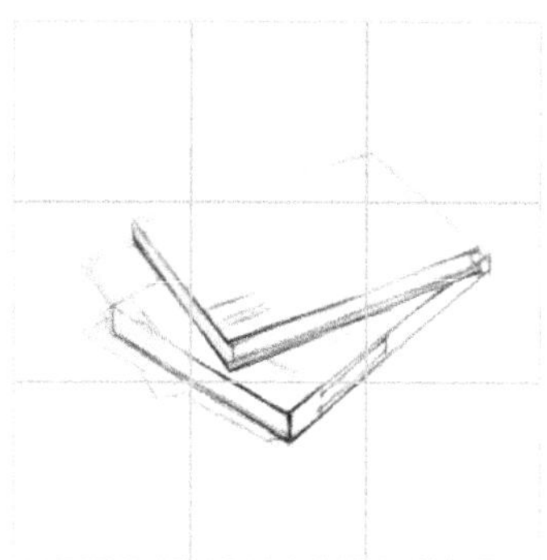

Sketch the general composition of the books.

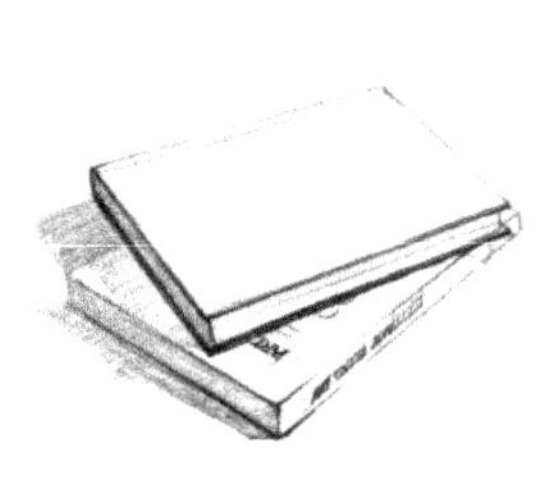

Identify the direction of the light source and shade in the general areas of shadow accordingly.

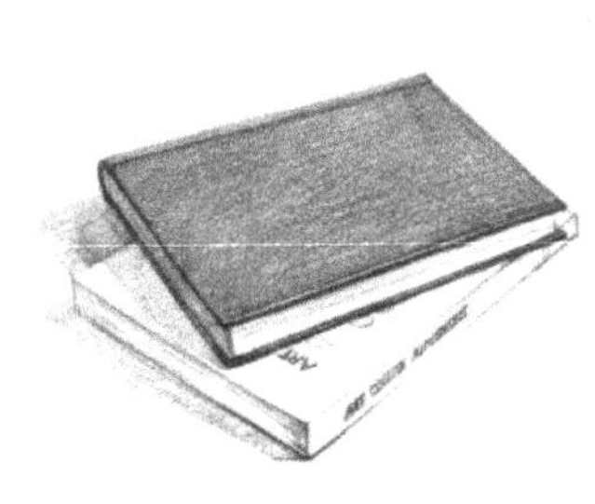

Continue to identify the darks, lights, and middle tones.

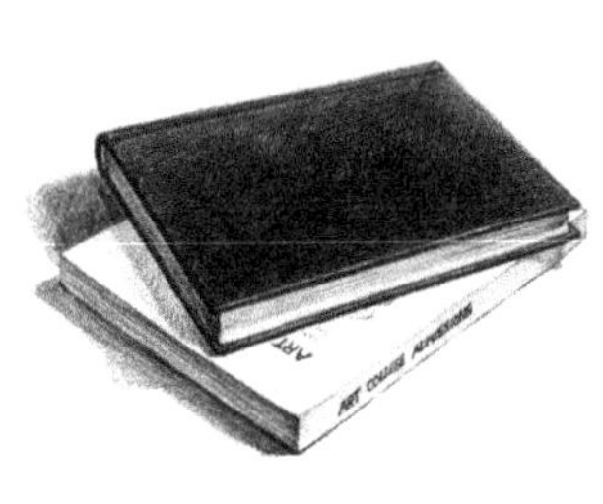

Make sure to use the entire range of tones to fully develop your drawing.

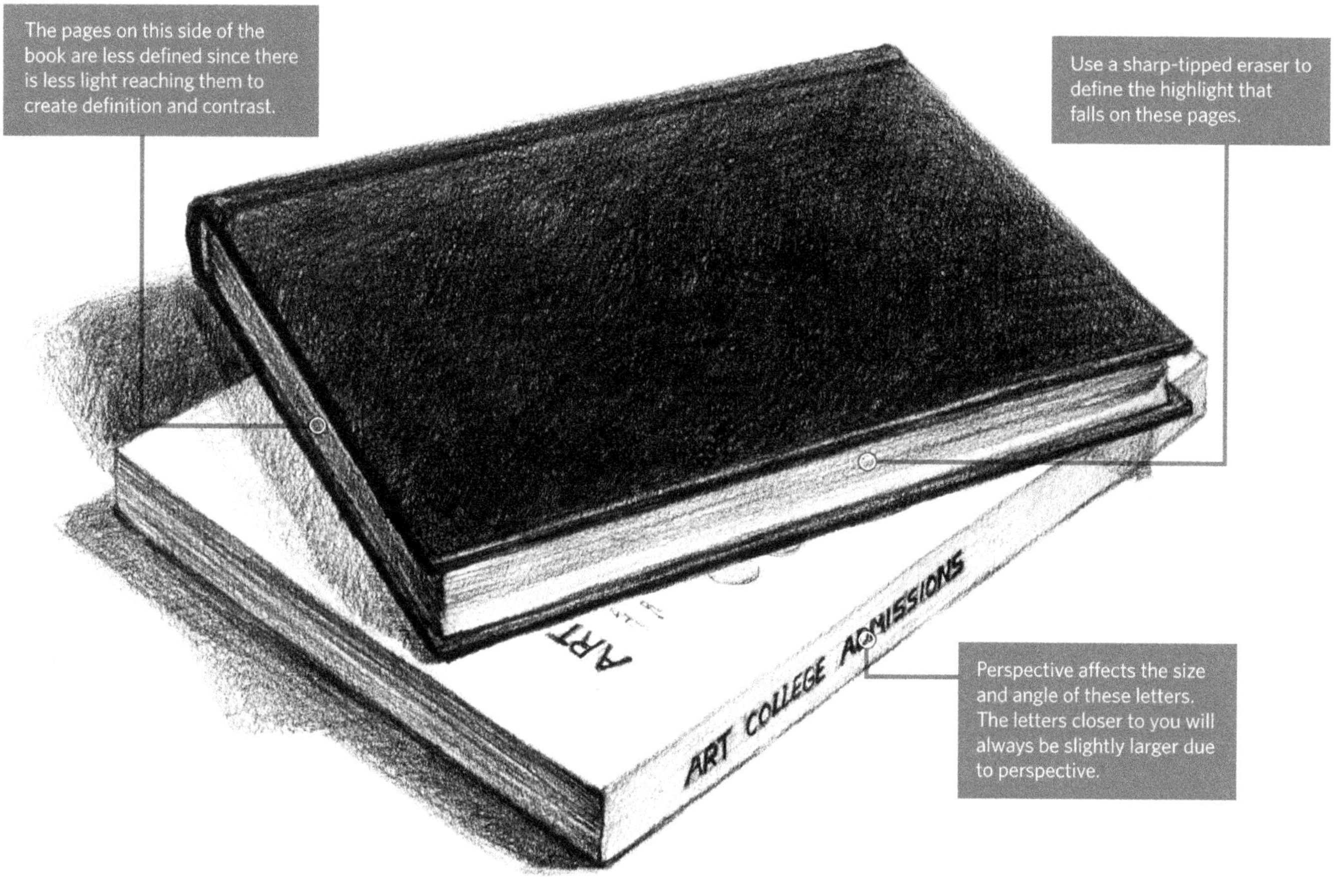

The pages on this side of the book are less defined since there is less light reaching them to create definition and contrast.

Use a sharp-tipped eraser to define the highlight that falls on these pages.

Perspective affects the size and angle of these letters. The letters closer to you will always be slightly larger due to perspective.

Now try drawing the books yourself.

Similar to the edges of the cube in the first exercise, keep the respective edges of the books parallel to one another. Keeping these edges parallel is key to rendering these objects in correct proportion and perspective to one another.

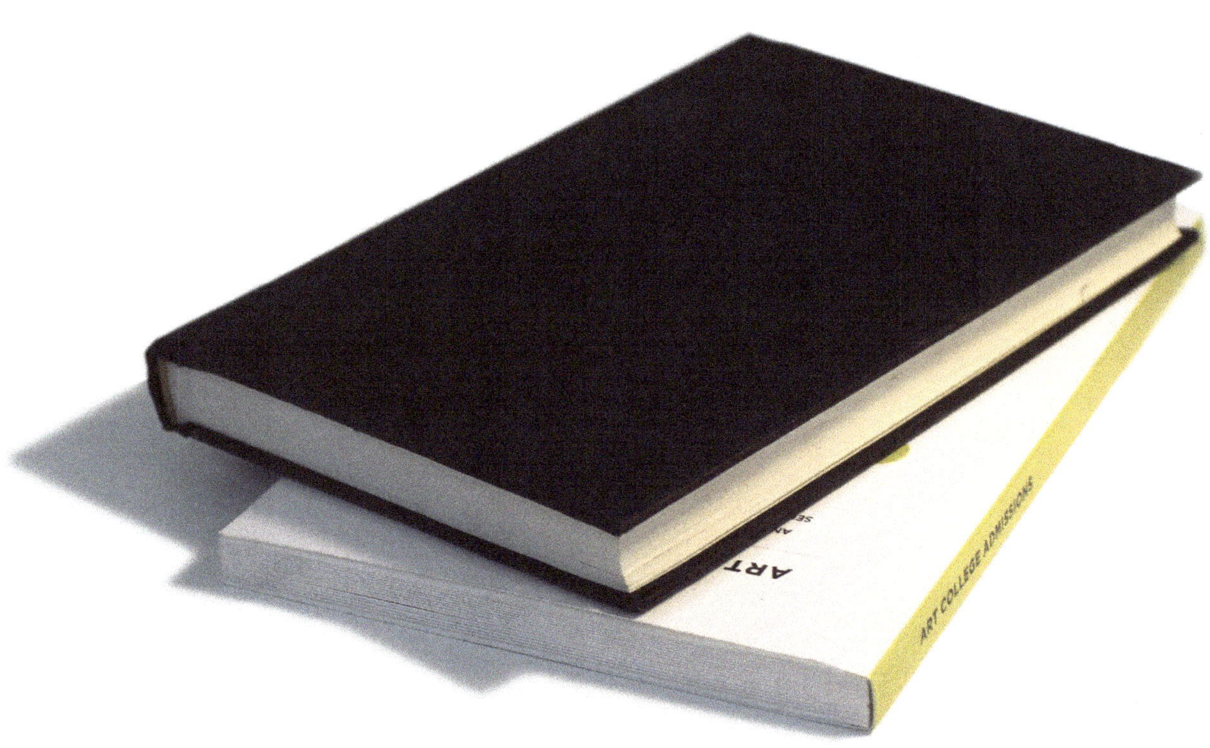

Now try drawing the books using the reference picture without any grid lines.

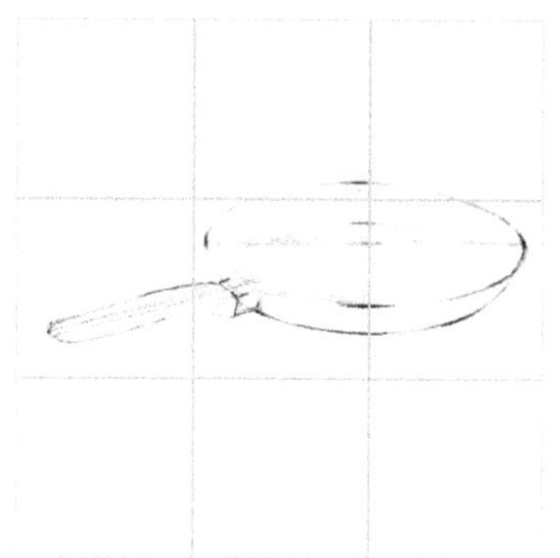

Sketch the general composition of the pan.

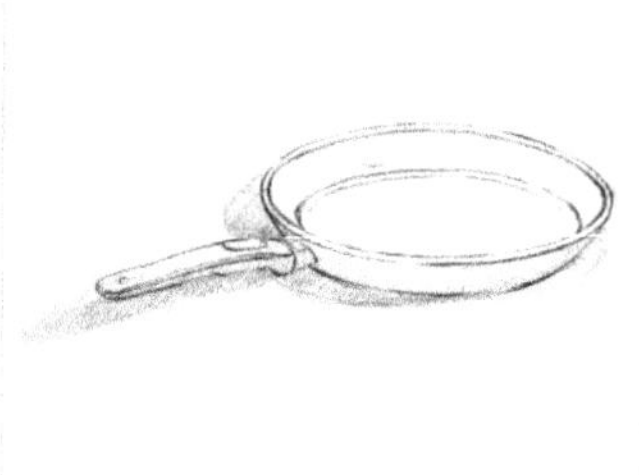

Identify the direction of the light source and shade in the general areas of shadow accordingly.

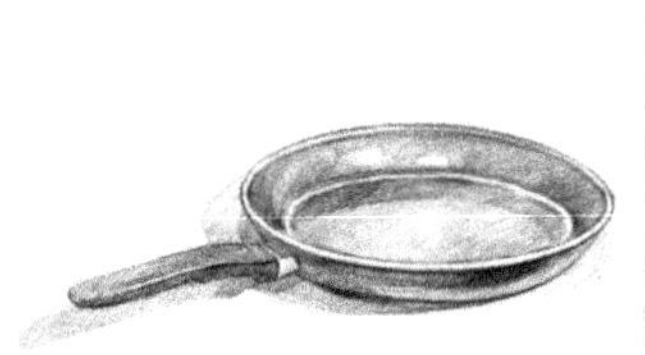

Continue to identify the darks, lights, and middle tones.

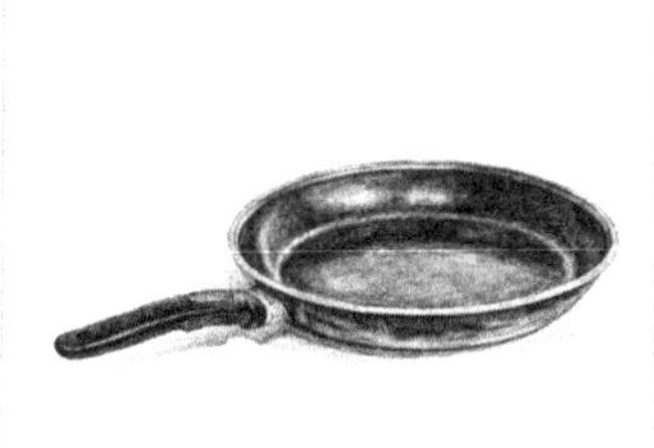

Make sure to use the entire range of tones to fully develop your drawing.

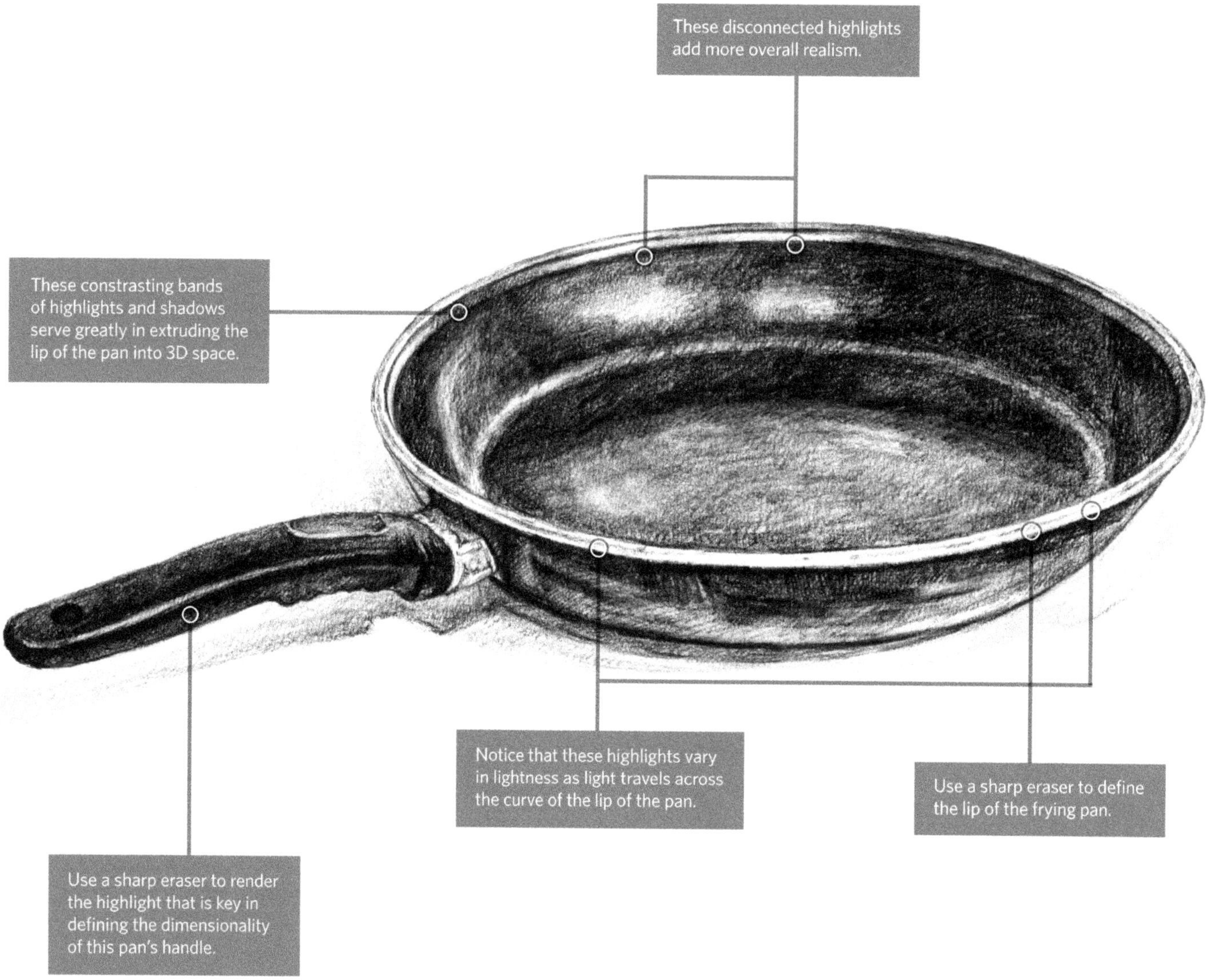

These disconnected highlights add more overall realism.

These constrasting bands of highlights and shadows serve greatly in extruding the lip of the pan into 3D space.

Notice that these highlights vary in lightness as light travels across the curve of the lip of the pan.

Use a sharp eraser to define the lip of the frying pan.

Use a sharp eraser to render the highlight that is key in defining the dimensionality of this pan's handle.

Now try drawing the frying pan yourself.

The frying pan is more difficult to render than a cup because it's shallower and the handle is longer, which adds more overall perspective to this piece. Pay close attention to the subtleties that define the pan's handle, its reflections on the bottom of the pan, and the main lip. Also, like the bowl, the side of shadow and light will be opposite inside the pan versus the outside of the pan. The more details you can capture, the more realistic the pan will appear, but make sure to work from general to detailed.

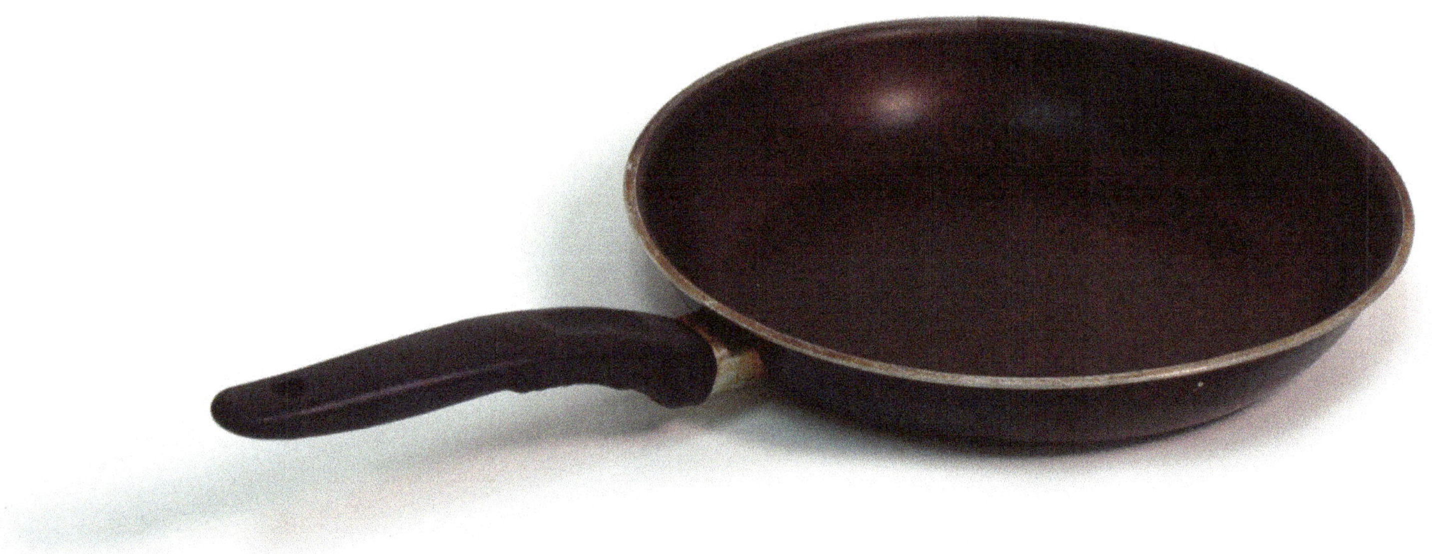

Now try drawing the frying pan using the reference picture without any grid lines.

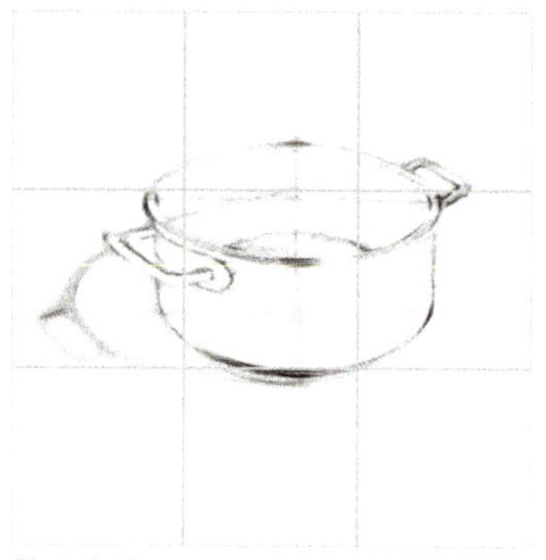

Sketch the general composition of the pot.

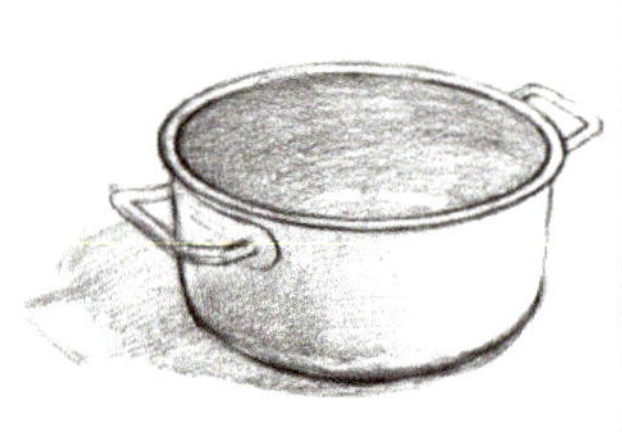

Identify the direction of the light source and shade in the general areas of shadow accordingly.

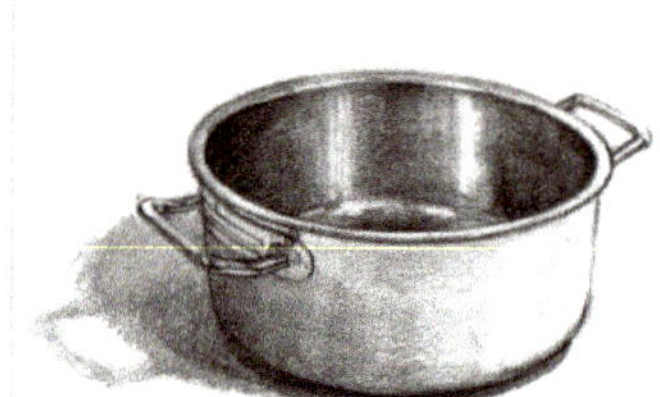

Continue to identify the darks, lights, and middle tones.

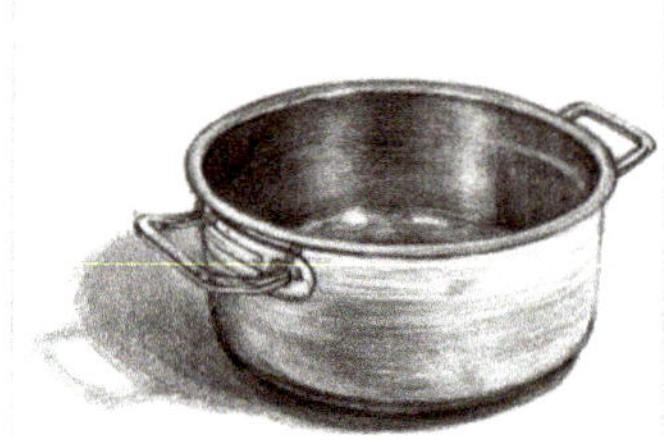

Make sure to use the entire range of tones to fully develop your drawing.

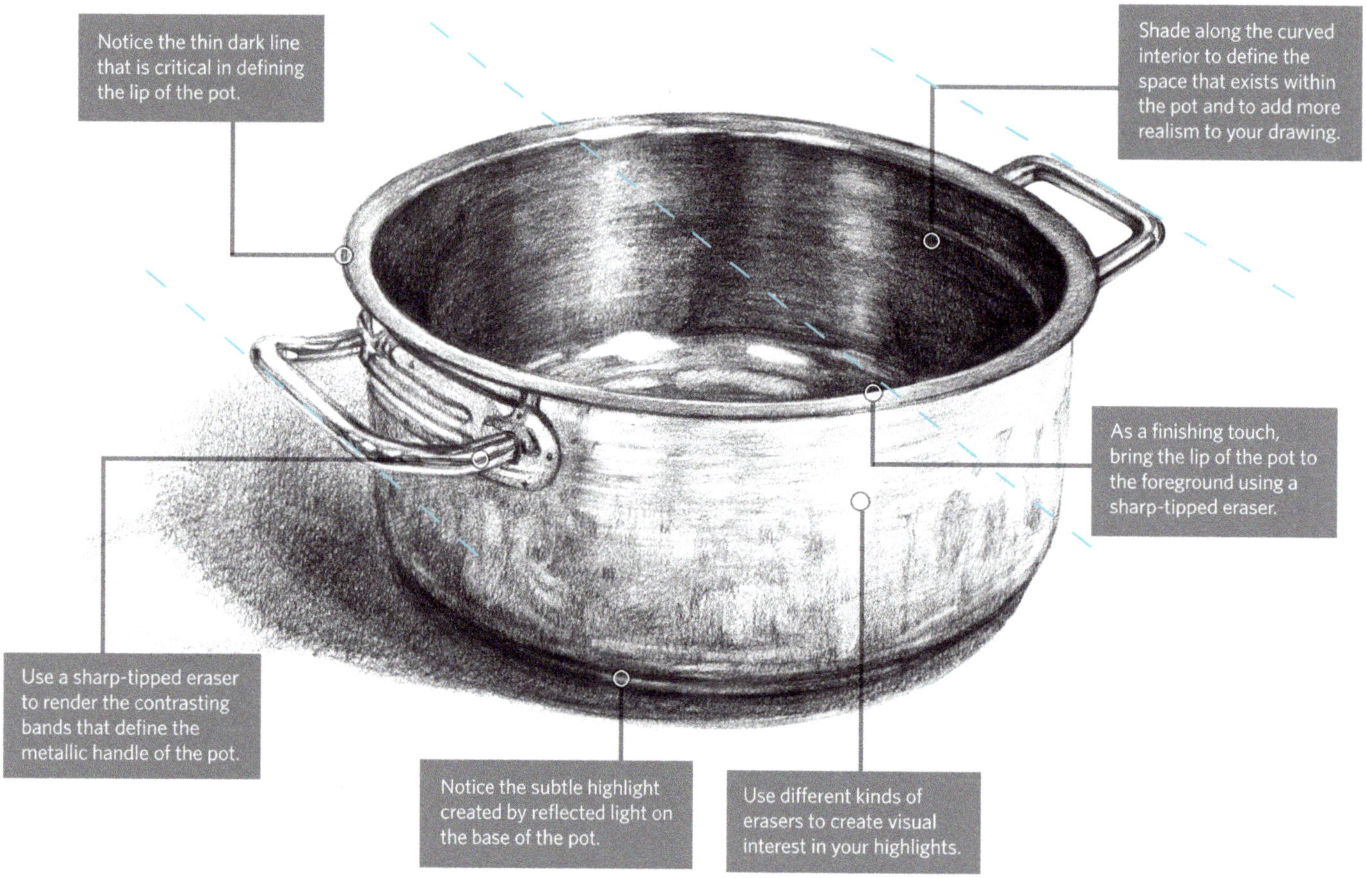

Notice the thin dark line that is critical in defining the lip of the pot.

Shade along the curved interior to define the space that exists within the pot and to add more realism to your drawing.

As a finishing touch, bring the lip of the pot to the foreground using a sharp-tipped eraser.

Use a sharp-tipped eraser to render the contrasting bands that define the metallic handle of the pot.

Notice the subtle highlight created by reflected light on the base of the pot.

Use different kinds of erasers to create visual interest in your highlights.

Now try drawing the metal pot yourself.

Drawing the pot will combine your skills from practicing with metal and from drawing the frying pan. Remember the inside of the pot will be darker than the outside, and pay attention to the bands of light on both the inside and outside. To properly capture the volume of the pot, make sure to render the sides using vertical motions, then go back into it using horizontal strokes that follow the shape of the pot. As always, work from general to specific.

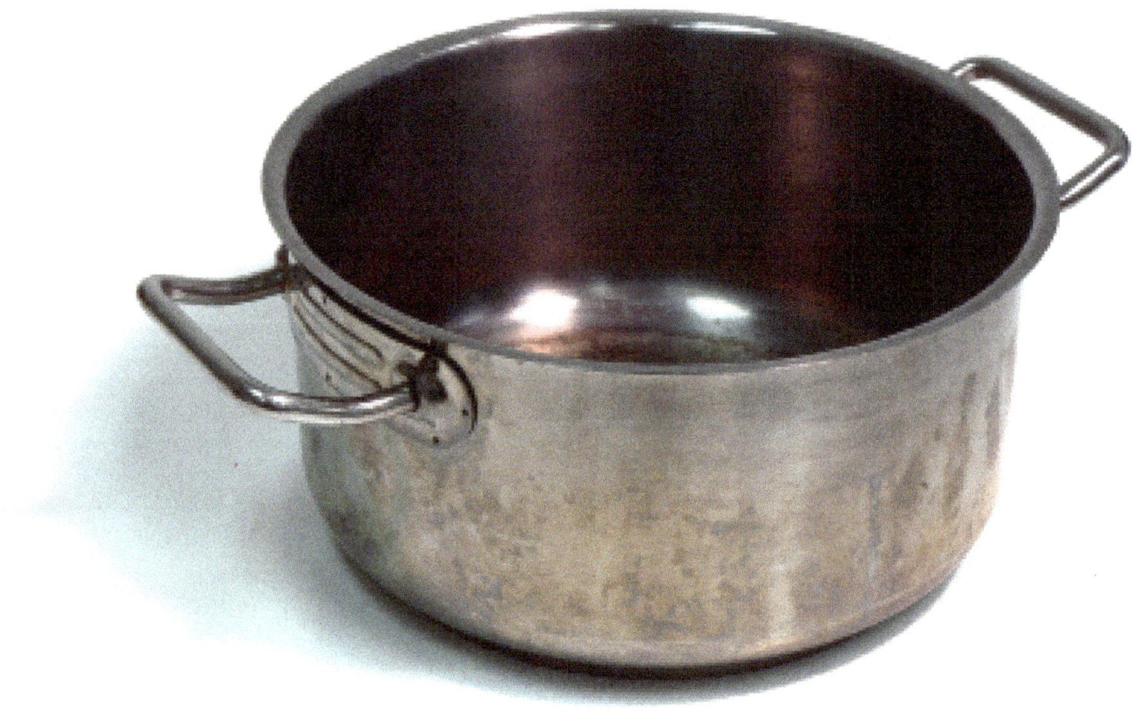

Now try drawing the metal pot using the reference picture without any grid lines.

ABOUT OOGIE HAUS

Oogie Haus is an art foundation unique for its diverse artistic endeavors, including an emphasis in art education, art & design internship opportunities, and volunteer outreach programs. There have been several book publications as well, such as "Art College Admissions," an insightful guideline for students applying to art schools.

Besides being an educational resource, Oogie Haus functions dually as an art gallery and art dealership. Through its research, it seeks to contribute a bigger network for local and international artists simultaneously curating its unique voice in todays art world. For more information please visit www.oogiehaus.com

ABOUT THE AUTHOR

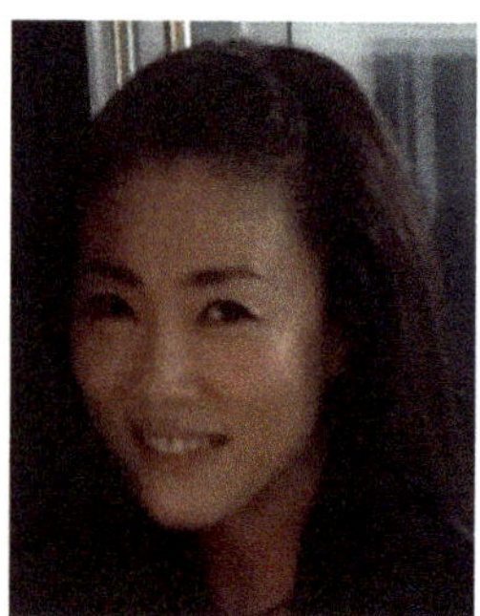

WOOK CHOI is an accomplished art dealer, education columnist, author, art educator, art gallerist, and art portfolio consultant who has guided over a thousand students to college admissions and scholarship success during the course of her 31-year teaching career.
She has received widespread recognition for her teaching methods from Mayor Michael Bloomberg; former First Lady Laura Bush; the New York Commissioner of Education, Richard P. Mills; US Congress member, Jerrold Nadler; the Alliance for Young Artists; YoungArts; and the Marie Walsh Sharpe Foundation. For more information, please visit www.wookchoi.com.

YOU CAN CONTINUE TO DEVELOP YOUR ARTISTIC SKILLS IN DIFFERENT MEDIA!

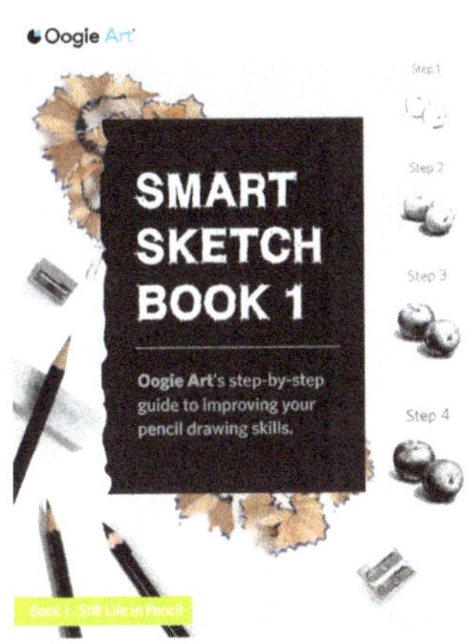

SMART SKETCHBOOK 1:
Still Life in Pencil

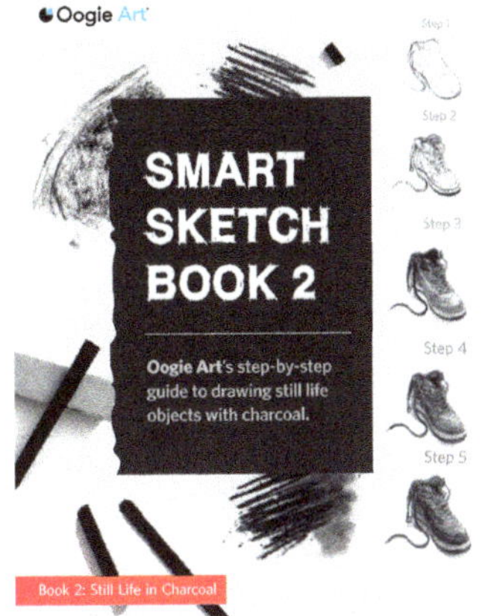

SMART SKETCHBOOK 2:
Still Life in Charcoal

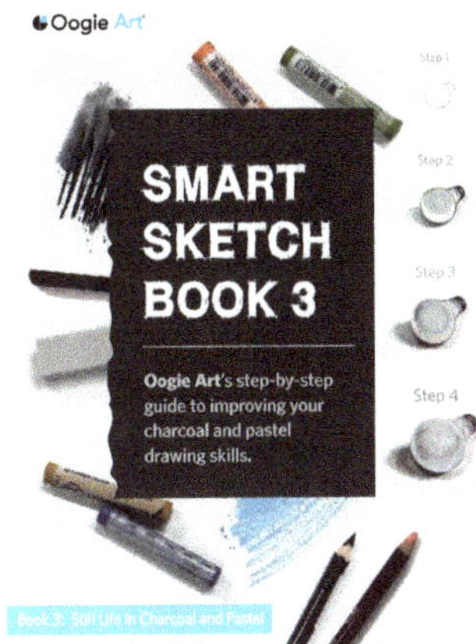

SMART SKETCHBOOK 3:
Still Life in Charcoal and Pastel

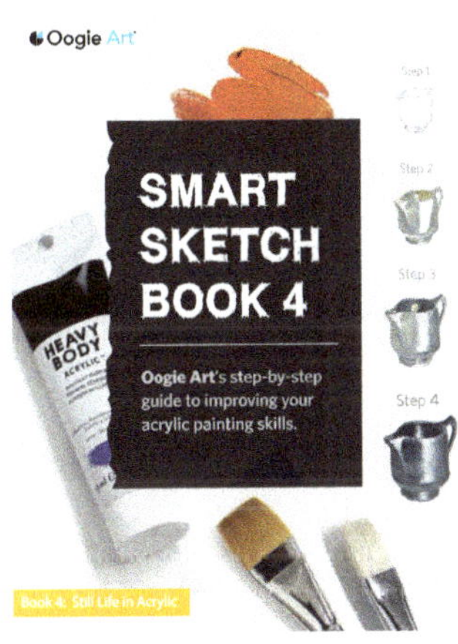

SMART SKETCHBOOK 4:
Still Life in Acrylic

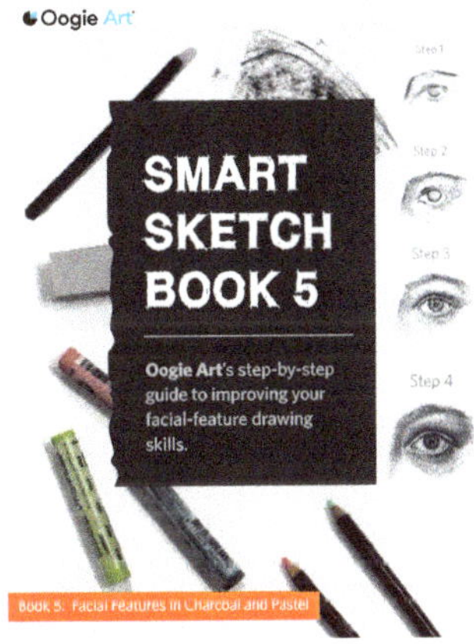

SMART SKETCHBOOK 5:
Facial Features in Charcoal and Pastel

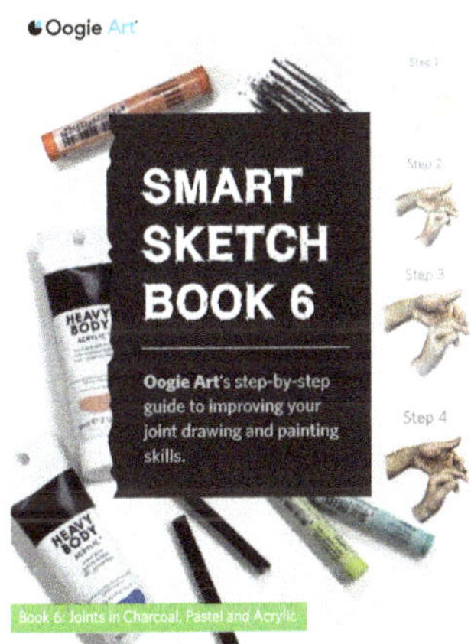

SMART SKETCHBOOK 6:
Joints in Charcoal, Pastel and Acrylic

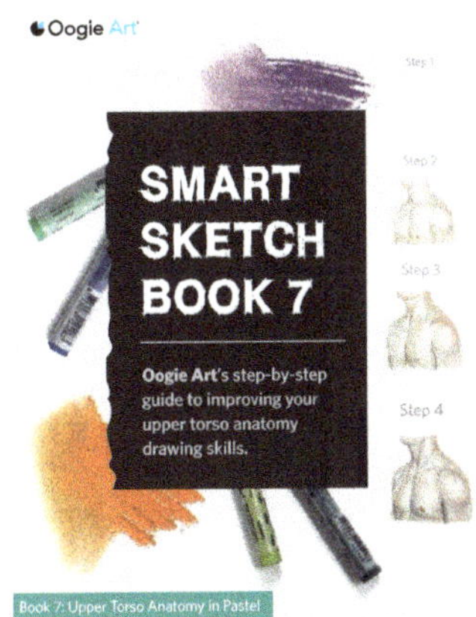

SMART SKETCHBOOK 7:
Upper Torso Anatomy in Pastel

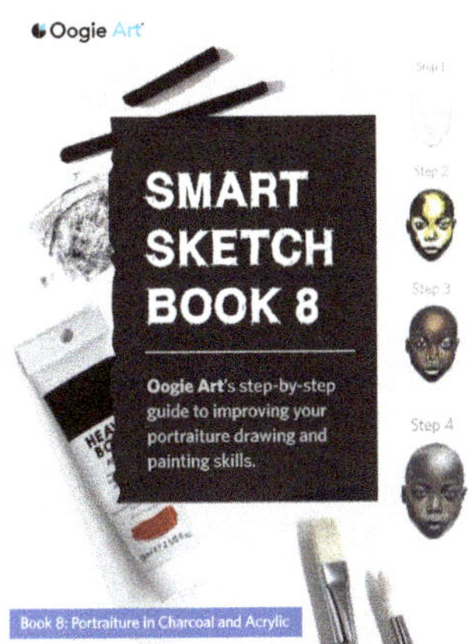

SMART SKETCHBOOK 8:
Portraiture in Charcoal and Acrylic

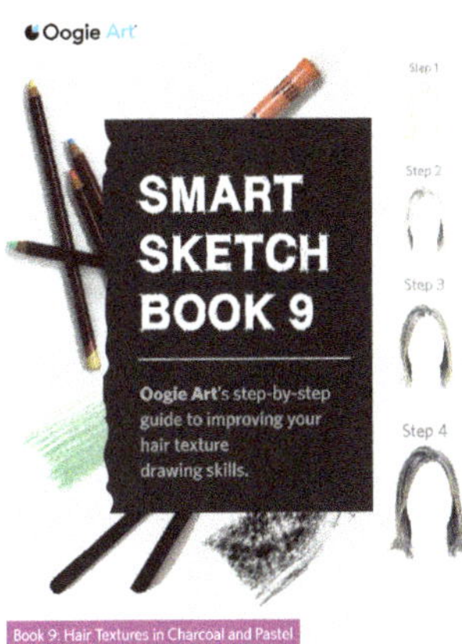

SMART SKETCHBOOK 9:
Hair Textures in Charcoal and Pastel

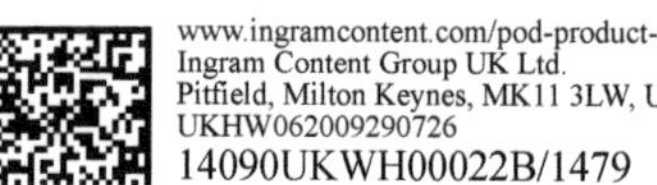
www.ingramcontent.com/pod-product-compliance
Ingram Content Group UK Ltd.
Pitfield, Milton Keynes, MK11 3LW, UK
UKHW062009290726
14090UKWH00022B/1479

9 780985 580926